£4.50

GW00871211

Gertrude
Hoeksema

REFORMED FREE
PUBLISHING ASSOCIATION
P.O. BOX 2006
GRAND RAPIDS, MI 49501

PRINTED IN THE UNITED STATES OF AMERICA

Lori

Preface

The Lord made Lori a special girl. He gave her special handicaps, multiple handicaps with which she struggled through her whole life. She was profoundly deaf, a near-mute, with paralysis on one side of her throat, mentally impaired, and a severe diabetic. The Lord let her live on the earth with us for twenty-four years.

During those years Lori was special to those who knew her. Her outgoing nature and spontaneous ways of showing her love drew her friends close. All who knew her counted her as a friend.

Although she lived in the small town of Byron Center in southwestern Michigan all her life, much of her story is set in the nearby small city of Hudsonville. She attended church at Hudsonville Protestant Reformed Church and it was Lori's pastor (and mine) who took the first steps toward making this story happen. He asked me to teach Bible lessons to four special teenage girls from the Hudsonville congregation. Lori was one of the girls.

The story of Lori concentrates on the last four years of her life, the years of her Bible classes. It was during those years that she had a spiritual awakening and an amazing spiritual growth. She was a simple and yet a profound girl. A lovely, sympathetic, intuitive girl, she expressed her responses to the surprising truths she discovered in her Bible lessons with faith and trust and love, straight from the depths of her heart. She was one of God's special children. God was her special friend, too.

Contents

Chapter 1

Tell Me About Lori

In was nine o'clock on a Monday evening in Room 3 of Hudsonville Protestant Reformed Church. Though it was a balmy autumn evening outside, my hands were icy and my heart was beating too fast. Any minute now, Lori would walk through the door, a Lori I did not know, a Lori who was deaf and mute. She would smile at me, I hoped, sit down, and we would start our class. I would teach her.

I thought I was prepared. The Bible lesson was in place. The visual aids and pictures we would use in class were neatly arranged. I *wanted* to teach her, I *longed* to teach her, but now I knew I wasn't ready. Maybe I would never be.

Then Lori walked in with a semblance of a smile on her face, and sat down. I smiled my warmest smile back and we started our first class together.

Why was I here in one of the classrooms of Hudsonville Church on October 25, 1982, to teach New Testament History to twenty-year-old Lori, who was not only deaf, who spoke very little, and who was also mentally impaired? How did I come to be here in Room 3 tonight?

I was here because of a simple question to our pastor on a spring evening the previous May. Pastor Van Baren and his wife, and my husband and I were having dinner together in a cozy corner of Bil-Mar Inn on the shore of Lake Michigan, and at the same time enjoying the sunset over Lake Michigan.

When we four went out for dinner together, we tried to find quiet, pleasant surroundings. It was our time to relax. Usually we did not talk shop on those evenings, the kind of shop-talk two ministers and wives discuss: busy schedules, church activities, heavy responsibilities. . . . But tonight was an exception. We talked about our church. My husband and I were fairly recent newcomers to our Hudsonville congregation and wanted to learn many more names and faces. Slowly our talk drifted to the make-up, the specific character of our Hudsonville congregation, and very naturally the subject of the handicapped children in our congregation came up.

"Do you think Hudsonville has more than the usual number of handicapped children?" my husband asked.

As we started naming the impaired children, I interrupted: "What can you tell me about the girl I see in the narthex every Sunday morning? She doesn't look very happy about going to church. She's the girl with the heavy step. I think she is deaf, and I suspect mentally impaired."

I went on. "The girl appeals to me, but I don't know quite how to approach her. I would like to be her friend."

Our pastor put down his fork and looked astounded. "You've been reading my mind?"

All three of us looked up at him at once, and I asked, "What do you mean: 'You've been reading my mind?' "

He must have had one of his ideas again. He had a reputation for good ideas. Was he going to try one on *me*? I supposed it would be something in the field of education.

For more than twenty years I had taught children, mostly young children, but through the years I had had contact with children of all ages. In March I had not signed my contract to teach another year. I would turn to other projects. Now it was May, and I felt a little apprehensive. Would I be happy without being surrounded with children? Would I miss them too much?

My education had prepared me to teach both gifted and handi-

2

capped children. Experience taught me that, especially with the children who were slow to learn, understanding, compassion, and encouragement — never say "can't" — were some of the best educational tools. These special children, who needed the extra smile, the extra nudge, the few minutes of special help at noon-hour, became truly special children in my life. Now I would not be teaching children. I would miss them.

The pastor's voice brought me from my reverie back to our topic of conversation. He was saying, "I'm glad we're having this leisurely dinner here tonight, because we can take our time to discuss the problems of the four older handicapped girls in our congregation. Our council wants to help them with spiritual instruction, if they can. The girls need help in Bible studies. Oh, they have had some Sunday School, but they've long outgrown that. And because of their impairments, they went to secular schools for special education and had little or no Bible classes at school."

Over the rest of our dinner, we all joined in a lively conversation about these girls: Glenda, Betty, Becky, and Lori, the four girls with varying degrees of disabilities, from mild to severe. Glenda needed a little extra help with doctrinal studies. Betty, a slow learner, had to be helped at her own pace. Becky, a dark-haired girl with Down's Syndrome, would be able to learn Bible stories and their meanings. Lori, a deaf-mute, would have to be taught with special methods, so she would learn with her *eyes.*

"They're too mature to learn with the younger children," one of us said.

"And they don't fit with high school girls with jobs and dates and driver's licenses."

Where *do* girls such as these go for more advanced spiritual training? If they cannot learn at the level of their peers, how do they learn Bible truths, except in special classes just for them?

For almost two hours we sat in our cozy spot overlooking the lake asking these and many more questions and trying to find the answers. Our pastor summed it up for us: "That's why I've been wanting to tell you what is in my mind. Trude, the council asks whether you will start Bible classes, probably one on one, for these four girls. Find out their needs and teach them accordingly. We will furnish you with any materials you need, and any advice, if we are able to give it."

What a challenge!

A piece of my delicious chicken sank down hard somewhere inside me. I swallowed, and said, "Tell me about Lori."

Chapter 2

Lori and Her Early Schooling

Nineteen years earlier Lori was born to Jay and Arla Holstege. She was the first child in the home of eighteen-year-old Arla. Some months before Lori was born, when the doctors had advised that Arla have abdominal surgery, they discovered that she was pregnant. Arla had surgery and recovered well, but after Lori was born prematurely, at four pounds and six ounces, the doctors told her that the surgery might have affected the baby adversely. When the young parents took her home, she was a tiny bundle weighing only four pounds.

They realized, slowly at first, that something was wrong with Lori. She grew, but did not respond as a normal baby does. Often parents are too close to a problem, concerned with feeding schedules, the health, and the growth of their baby, especially their first baby, to be able to pin-point the exact problem of their child. Relatives of Lori began to see that all was not well with this tiny girl. Although she seemed content and rather happy, her face did not have a typical baby's smile. It was a crooked smile, and her lips seemed to be too stiff to smile the way other babies smiled. Her parents saw Lori's problems, too.

Before she was a year old, they *knew* something was wrong. She did not scare at noises, she was not developing normally, and she had a very small head.

When she was fifteen months old, Lori gave her parents a shocking scare. She suddenly vomited blood, and continued to vomit blood. After rushing her to the hospital, they waited to learn what dreadful illness Lori had; but the doctors in Grand Rapids could find no cause. Although Lori broke out in a rash, which they said might be chicken pox, and could be the cause of her problem, they discharged her without a firm diagnosis of her trouble.

Not satisfied, her parents took her to the Mayo Clinic at

Rochester, Minnesota. There the diagnosis of little Lori's throwing up blood was not any more specific: the doctors at Mayo Clinic said she would outgrow her problem. Their diagnosis was correct. She did outgrow it. Meantime, they kept her in the hospital four or five days for other tests. Their prognosis was that she would be retarded, and that her retardation would worsen. They told Lori's parents that they based many of their findings on her small head size. Although the doctors found Lori to be retarded, they said nothing about possible deafness. With that gloomy picture of Lori's future life, her discouraged parents took their baby home.

When she was two years old, they were still not satisfied that they had an accurate picture of Lori's troubles. Was she deaf? Mildly retarded? Severely retarded? Her parents needed more help and advice. They decided to take her to the Philadelphia Institute for the Severely Handicapped. After the doctors there tested Lori extensively, they gave somewhat the same diagnosis: Lori was a severely handicapped child. Her parents weren't sure. Living with Lori every day, while they still suspected that she was profoundly deaf, they knew that she could learn some things. They knew she needed her home environment. Although she had never tried to talk, at age two she walked!

When Lori was three years old, her parents, acting on their conviction that she was deaf, enrolled her as a part-time student at Shawnee Park School for the Deaf. But they were not convinced that they had the answer to Lori's problems. Was she partially deaf, totally deaf, somewhat retarded, or severely retarded? Still looking for answers, they took her for testing, particularly for testing her intelligence, to Henry Ford Hospital in Detroit. They went when she was four years old and again when she was five. Both times she was judged to have normal intelligence. The reason she tested as a child of average intelligence, the personnel at the hospital told her parents, was that she had some very high scores and some very low. These scores averaged out to give a picture of a girl with normal intelligence. Her high scores were in the areas of comprehension, and her low scores in areas of co-ordination. She seemed to be a child of opposites.

Somewhat encouraged, her parents wanted to take the next step for her education, some type of special education. When she was five, she was tested by the Grand Rapids Public School System, in preparation for placing her in the proper area for her needs. This time she was diagnosed as *aphasic*, without the ability of articulate speech, due to brain damage.

What were these poor, confused parents to do now? Was she severely retarded, ready to be institutionalized, or of normal intelligence, with some highs and some lows? Was she deaf? Or aphasic? If the experts did not know what was wrong with their little girl, nor how to treat her, and could not agree on methods of educating her, how would they know the best way to follow for Lori's education? What did their little girl think of all the testing and uncertainty? What a strain and confusion all this testing and experimenting with various methods to correct a nebulous handicap must have been for the little five-year-old! Another serious aspect of the problem was that Lori was losing many precious years of consistent schooling particularly suited to her specific handicap: profound deafness.

If Lori must have special education, her parents wanted her to be taught in a Christian environment. They turned their thoughts to Elim Christian School in the Chicago suburb of Palos Heights, established for Christian education of handicapped children, and with an excellent reputation for successfully teaching deaf children. When she was six years old, Lori's parents drove her to Chicago, and introduced her to Elim. They saw her settled in her room in a pleasant environment, with a caring and dedicated staff of teachers and aides. Then, with heavy hearts, they left her there for two weeks. Every other week for the next three years, they drove to Chicago from their home in the Grand Rapids suburb of Byron Center to get Lori for the weekend. Lori could hardly wait for these weekends, especially because she had a new baby brother, Randy. She played with him and mothered him during her happy weekend, and was reluctant to leave him when it was time to go back to Elim. All through her life, Lori and Randy retained their closeness.

She had a hard time adjusting to Elim at first, and was often troublesome for the teachers and helpers, especially after her visits with her family. In her short life she had been taken to so many strange places, seen so many unfamiliar faces, and was examined by dozens of pairs of different hands. Now she had lost the security of her home, her parents, her sister Debbie, a year younger than she was, and her baby brother. She was put in a totally strange environment, with entirely different rules. Lori rebelled. In her silent world, she could not understand why she lived among strangers: and her outbursts of temper, which the kindly teachers understood, showed everyone her extreme displeasure. Although she could not understand why she was at Elim, nor communicate very effectively, and although she was taught as an aphasic, not a deaf girl, Lori gradually adjusted to Elim. With loving and firm care, her dedicated teachers helped her to adjust to the routine and the learning at Elim, and she began to love her home away from home. She progressed well, learned many skills, and began to learn to read some words.

Lori had trouble mastering the written and spoken word. But

already at Elim, Lori showed a quick grasp of spacial relation-ships. She was especially sharp in knowledge of geography, and she applied her skills to her life, especially to her travels with her parents. She began to make her parents aware, by gestures, that she knew where she was. Once, when they had taken a little side-trip with Lori before they took her back to Elim and were approaching it from an opposite direction, where Lori had not been before, she became very excited and let her parents know that they were almost at her school!

After three years of schooling for Lori at Elim, her parents were tired of the bi-weekly trips in all kinds of weather. Besides, they had two children at home. Although Lori *did* love Elim, her distress at saying good-bye to her parents every other week and being left there, a lonely, unhappy little girl, caused in-creasing trauma to them all. So her parents, with the advice of their pastor, decided to keep her at home and educate her in Grand Rapids. For the next year, Lori had a private tutor, who taught her as an aphasic.

Wasn't Lori deaf? Why did the experts think she should be taught as an aphasic? If she was profoundly deaf, she should be taught by other methods. An accurate diagnosis of her problem was long overdue. Desperate for an answer to Lori's problems, her parents tried one more avenue: they took her to Pine Rest Christian Hospital. The doctor there advised that they institu-tionalize her because of her disabilities. They *could not* take that advice. They knew, by living with her and training her, that Lori had some potential. But they must know the methods to use before they would see progress.

When Lori was nine, her parents, still convinced that deafness played a large part in Lori's handicap, took her to the Institute of the Deaf in St. Louis, Missouri. There she was diagnosed, with certainty, to be profoundly deaf. In her tests there, Lori showed that she was mentally only slightly below an average nine-year-old.

At last they knew! Lori's parents were relieved and encouraged. There would be no more talk of institutionalizing their dear child. And she *could* learn.

Their next trip was to Flint, Michigan, to have Lori evaluated for communication. Would it be signing or lip-reading? The specialists at the institute in Flint discouraged signing. Lori would not be quick enough to spell. She could not visualize a word and form each letter successively with quick fingers, for she lacked finger coordination and dexterity. Lori *could* learn, but not quickly. She was a slow, plodding girl.

Back in Grand Rapids, her parents enrolled her in Shawnee Park School, where Lori learned to read by pictures and by lip-reading. For communication, the teachers at Shawnee used the lip-reading technique, along with gestures. She began to read lips fairly well, and the teachers aimed at the goal of teaching Lori to speak. They hoped that some day she might talk. But, in the Lord's plan, that was never to be. Her small motor muscles were impaired, resulting in an under-development on one side of her throat, which prevented her from forming words clearly enough to be understood. Lori said, or tried to say, some words, but she tended to slide a two-syllable word into one, or to distort some of the sounds. She was always willing to *try* to say a word, but would rather use gestures. She developed her own brand of signing. Her family helped her with a satisfactory method of signs and gestures, and they communicated rather easily.

Later Lori went on to Iroquois Junior High, where she attended classes for the deaf. She graduated from Ottawa Hills High School, in special education, and then went on to Kent Occupational High School.

Lori's early life was also plagued with physical problems. Twice when she was very young, she broke an arm. She was hospitalized for nephritis when she was five. And then one morning when she was eleven, she did not feel very well when she left for school. Her mother worried about her all day. Not only had she been drinking too many liquids lately, but her heritage was against her. There was diabetes in the family. Arla's father had died from it. That day Arla went to buy dye sticks for testing a diabetic, and as soon as Lori came home from school, still not feeling well, she tested her. The test was so positive that Lori was immediately hospitalized. And she had insulin shots twice a day for the rest of her life.

Both parents and child must have had unsettled feelings in these early years. The Lord had given them a child with multiple handicaps, physical and mental, a child who needed special care and special education. Yet confusion about her training and schooling became almost a way of life for the Holsteges, because it seemed no one knew quite what to do with this unique little girl.

Chapter 3

Lori With Her Family

From the time Lori was tiny, her family and her relatives always talked to her, although they were almost sure she could not understand. When they talked with her, she did not seem to respond normally. She was usually fairly content and happy as a child, but she never smiled. When her family easily communicated with one another and she sat by in perplexity and confusion, she *must* have known she was living in a communicating world. Especially in later life, when she tried to communicate, and expressed her joy with rather loud outbursts of laughter, she sensed that her outburst was too loud, and covered her mouth, with a gleam still left in her eyes.

Lori was eleven months old when her sister Debbie was born. Randy was born while she was a student at Elim, and Tracy came when Lori was having a party on her ninth birthday. After that, Tracy was *her* baby. Randy and Debbie, who grew up with this silent sister, assumed from earliest childhood that Lori was deaf; and as children so often do, they easily adjusted to her handicap. Gestures did as well as words, and they invented their own system of sign language as they played. Lori was energetic, almost hyper-active, and she wanted to join in all the fun around her. Her brother and sisters did not think of her as very handicapped. She always joined in the games with zest: hide and seek, softball, and later basketball, bike riding, sledding, and swimming. They grew accustomed to having her along, and helped her compensate for — and overcome — some of the problems her handicaps brought her.

She was always a sociable girl. She *liked* people, and she wanted people to *like* her. If Lori wanted extra attention, she almost forced her presence on those around her, trying to form words, but usually ending with unintelligible sounds. She loved to walk next door to Aunt Marcia and "talk" with her. Aunt Marcia, her father's brother's wife, was Lori's out-going and sympathetic friend, who took time to make Lori happy. When Aunt Marcia was busy, Lori looked at picture books by the hour, probably learning a lot from them, and interspersed her moments of quietness with spontaneous hugs and kisses for Aunt Marcia. It was the most fun to go to Aunt Marcia's house if Tom was home. The youngest child in the family, Tom had also had physical problems when he was young. He had been to the Mayo Clinic, and so had Lori. That was their common bond. He loved her, but when she ran over to his house to get his attention and keep it, he often thought of her as a gregarious little pest, and his love was tempered with gruffness and impatience. As they grew older, Tom was gentle and sympathetic, and Lori responded by showering him with affection. Tom's name was one of her easiest words to say, and she said it often and loudly as she ran across the yard to talk with him.

There were times of severe frustration for both Lori and her family when she was young. Energetic and head-strong, she wanted things to go *her* way. Her parents could not set her down somewhere and make her listen to reason; and they could not scold her, for she could not understand words. Sometimes they had to subdue her by force when she threw a temper tantrum. At times they gave in to her. Debbie, especially, gave in. She was almost the same age as Lori, and understood, probably more than the rest of the family, the frustrations and disappointments of her handicapped sister. One of Lori's grandmas solved the temper problem by putting her in a large closet alone until she simmered down. If the family checked on her, they found her sitting on the floor, with the light on, engrossed in the books stored there. After Lori began to learn to read words, and her family and friends could reason with her on paper, her tantrums and head-strong outbursts lessened.

In her early teen-age years, Lori and her family went through some difficult times. Lori knew she was the oldest of the four children, and when her parents went away, *she* wanted to rule the younger children, instead of listening to Debbie, whom her parents had put in charge. Even though the gap between Lori and her siblings was widening as she became older, and her development did not keep pace with her chronological age, she fought the rule, and argued it, and became angry about it. Then after she had had her say to her brother and sisters, sometimes with violence, she realized that she *could not* be in charge, and she was very, very sorry. She then busied herself the rest of the time of her parent's absence kissing and making up and being friends again.

Even in these trying times, both for Lori and for her family, there was a gradual acceptance of the Lord's will. They lived and coped with her problems, taking a day at a time; they did the best they could for her each day, and tried not to worry about her future and theirs.

Lori drew friends to herself like a magnet. No one had to teach her that the way to have friends was to *be* one. She loved her family with sincere affection, and she was always ready to show it. Her sisters and brother saw a Lori who was usually happy: a giving, loving, affectionate girl. She never went to sleep without kissing each member of the family, even if she read too long in bed, past their bedtimes, and she had to wake them for the evening ritual.

She was always sociable. Her relatives could not help showering her with affection, because *her* affection was so spontaneous. And when she was sad or quiet because of her handicap, or rebelled and had a tantrum, she would cheer up if friends came and she could show off. Despite her growing loss of coordination, on outings she was the family clown. Because she could not water-ski, she sat on an inner-tube behind a boat. She made sure everyone was watching her, and then clowned as she was towed across the lake. Her sense of humor, with a bit of showmanship, never failed to entertain her family and friends.

Often on Sunday mornings after church services, she went with her family to Grandpa and Grandma Holstege. After grandma served refreshments, and Lori made sure she visited with each relative, she went to look at the birthday calendar in grandma's kitchen. It was the one with all the circles. Lori circled the birthdays and anniversaries of all her relatives and acquaintances; and each year she could add more circles to the calendar, as she found more friends. When she finished looking at her calendar, she would often disappear into grandmother's big closet, turn on the light, and pore over recipe books or knitting books. These seemingly dull books were so interesting to her that she was unaware of what was going on in the rest of the house. One Sunday Lori's family were already on their way home, when someone noticed that she was missing. They turned around, and when they came back to grandmother's house, Lori was still serenely looking at knitting books, oblivious, of course, to all the noises of her family's departure.

Lori had a generous nature. She loved to *give.* Why? Not to buy friends, because she already had them; but to be kind to them, to show them love. One day in her early teens, she took some money from home and gave it to her friends at school. Her brother and sisters found out, and when she was confronted at home with her theft, she realized it was wrong to steal money

even if her motives for its use had seemed right to her; and she was very sorry. Gradually she learned to control her impulses and she always kept her friends.

Lori wrote notes and letters to her friends, telegraph-style: in clipped form, using only the important words in the message, and leaving the rest to the understanding of the reader. And her friends wrote her back. Getting personal mail was one of her greatest joys in life. Lori wrote many notes such as the following to her friends:

> Dear Kandi,
> On June summer I over sleep at Kandi house at time 12:30 p.m. Yes No circle Kandi will come to Sunday Protestant Reformed Byron Center Christian Jr. High 9:30 a.m. 5:00 p.m. Lori loves Kandi — friends I prayed to Kandi.

Kandi knew what this little note meant, because she knew Lori. It meant that if Lori wanted to sleep over at a friend's house, she loved to come early in the day (12:30 p.m.). And this note (written a little later in her life when she belonged to the new Byron Center congregation) gave her friend Kandi clear directions as to time and place. In her last sentence Lori was having her usual troubles with prepositions. She prayed *for* Kandi, as she did for all her friends. Her friends didn't mind Lori's telegraph-style notes. Because they knew her, they could unscramble them and understand them. They treasured them.

As she grew older and could not be considered a little girl any longer, the gap between her and her brother and sisters widened. Lori realized she was being left behind and knew how great her handicap was. They could take drivers' training. They could be independent, earn money, and spend it. Lori could not. And she never learned the value of money. But one of the saddest things in her life was the realization that she would never use the telephone. She would have loved it! Of course, she tried to use it. She knew the telephone numbers of all her friends, and she called them, lay on the floor with her feet up, as teenagers are supposed to do, and chatted with them in her broken sounds. None of her friends minded, because it was *Lori!*

* * * * * * * * * * * * * * * * * * *

Lori was born into a Christian home. When she was little, she joined her family when they had devotions at mealtimes, but she sat in complete silence. She learned to sit still. Her family did not know what was going on in her mind. They could not know because she could not tell them. Did she understand what these devotions were, and did she know what the Bible reading was? Her parents taught her to fold her hands and close her eyes when they all prayed together, and her mother tried to teach her a bed-time prayer. Did she understand that she was praying to God? Or was it just a ritual to her?

What was Lori's understanding of spiritual things? Did the Lord give her insights into the mysteries of the spiritual realm? Her family could not know the answer. Though they tried to teach her in a childlike way about God, her family thinks that at that time she understood very little, and that her religious training was mainly formal. She went through the motions.

On the other hand, we cannot estimate the work of the Spirit in her little heart by our earthly standards. And we may never underestimate it. Lori moved her lips during prayer. Was she imitating her family or was she praying? Only the Lord knows.

When she was four years old, her parents sent her to a Bible class for handicapped children, and at Elim she was given some simple Bible instruction, but Lori probably did not recognize the Bible as God's Word during the first part of her life.

And she hated to go to church. She had to sit still in a complete vacuum for an hour to an hour and a half because, although she knew it had something to do with God, she did not understand just *why* she was attending church. She occupied herself with watching her friends and with writing, but she often put up a fuss when Sundays came. And she could be a glum little girl in church. Her family did not really know if she understood the meaning of going to church.

18

In her congregation at Hudsonville, Michigan, where she attended most of her life, she had many friends. Many of them, also the pastor and the elders in the council, observed her unhappiness at the church services which meant so little to her because she did not understand. The reason had to be her lack of spiritual training. But no one seemed to know how to give her lessons in Bible history nor to teach spiritual realities to a girl who seemed quite retarded and who was both deaf and mute. No one dared to teach her, and no one tried to give her the lessons she needed.

Chapter 4

Lori's First Lessons

It was October of 1982, and time for an exciting new venture: a challenging and a frightening venture. Following our long dinner conversation the previous May, our pastor worked with the council and me; and the plans to start classes with the four older handicapped girls were complete. I was to teach these four girls, with their varying degrees of problems. The first thing to do was set up conferences with the parents of the girls. Lori's mother came alone, and I had many questions to ask her, for at that time Lori was a stranger to me. I did not yet know her background nor her childhood history. I asked questions such as: How well can Lori read? Does she understand Who our God is? Has she ever read the Bible? Does she know how to pray? Does she know what sin is, and against Whom she sins? Her mother could not answer my questions because she did not know the answers, so our conference ended in my agreeing to take a step in the dark, and in trying to stumble along until I knew Lori better and had the answers to my questions.

We scheduled classes for Monday evening in Room 3 at Hudsonville Church. I would teach Betty at six, Becky at seven, Glenda at eight, and Lori at nine. It was not an ideal time for Lori, but Randy and Tracy also had catechism on that evening, and transportation problems were solved if Lori came at nine. On Monday, October 25, we would have our first class.

As nine o'clock neared, my hands turned icy cold and my heart beat too fast. Was Lori as apprehensive as I? I found out later, when I knew her well, that she wasn't. I had tried to prepare for this first lesson by calling her teachers at Shawnee and also at Kent Occupational High School, where she was attending at present. "What can I expect?" I asked. "What is her reading level?" The teachers told me that she read at a first grade — possibly early second grade level. She was a very loveable girl, they said, eager to please, willing and able to learn, up to a point.

Abstract concepts were beyond her. If that were true, how could I teach her concepts such as sin, forgiveness, grace, salvation? Would she understand that God is a Spirit?

I had asked her parents whether she knew and retained any Bible stories. She knew some stories, they said, especially those about Jesus. Several years earlier Lori had attended after-school Bible classes for deaf children taught by one of the teachers at Shawnee Park School. The teacher used gestures and flannel-graph illustrations, but the stories were very simple. Lori's parents were not sure that she had grasped them nor retained them. These facts did not give me enough information to use in planning.

So I drew up my own plans and decided on my own methods, but felt as if I were on shaky ground. I was very uncertain how my plans would work in practice. Before I left home, I voiced my fears to my husband. He encouraged me.

"You can't do it alone," he said. "Don't try. God's Spirit will work in her heart and make her understand much more than all your efforts. Do your best and leave it to the Lord."

And I did.

At nine o'clock Lori walked into Room 3 with a semblance of a smile, or at least a pleasant look on her face. I introduced myself by giving her a card saying, "I am Mrs. Hoeksema." I touched her to get her attention, she watched my lips as I said my name, and she tried to repeat it, not very successfully. Then she told me by sounds and gestures who had taken her to class and what vehicle they rode in, but I could understand only the driving gesture and the sweep of her arms, for distance, I supposed. We had a long way to go.

We began our lesson with prayer. I had typed a simple prayer on a four by six index card: and Lori and I made it a consistent pro-

cedure in all our future lessons to use four by six cards for our
prayers. It was a simple prayer, to make Lori aware of the great
God to Whom we were praying, the God Who made the heaven,
our earth, and us, too. In our prayer we asked for God's help in
our lesson, and for His Spirit in our hearts. She said, "um,"
and pointed toward her heart. She understood. At the *Amen,*
she clasped my hands, and that became a ritual for each lesson:
we clasped hands for the *Amen,* and said it aloud together.

We sat next to one another at a long table, where my visual aids
and a small eighteen by twenty-four inch communication chalkboard were spread, and we set to work. For all four girls, I had
decided to start our lessons with Jesus' public ministry. My purpose was to lead them, through the teachings of Jesus' life, to
the gospel of salvation; and I prepared the same subject matter
four different ways for my girls. Lori's lesson was the most
simple. I doubted whether she knew that the Bible is God's
Word; and that Word had to speak to her. But it was necessary
to bring that Word to her slowly and simply at first.

Together Lori and I started reading the lesson which I had typed
for her. It was the story of John the Baptist, from Matthew 3.

23

Because I did not know her reading level, I wrote a simple story of the preaching of John and of Jesus' baptism in the Jordan River by John. I used pictures to help her understand. Before we read the story proper, I asked a question on the communication board: "Lori, do you know what *sin* is?"

Could she understand a concept such as sin? I had to know. If she did not know, I had plans to try to teach her what sin is. She took the chalk from the ledge of the communication board, hesitated, and wrote, "bad — mad — temper," and graphically demonstrated those concepts. She made her face the picture of stubbornness, clenched her fist, and stamped. We laughed. It probably relieved the tension for both of us.

Now for the next concept: "Do you know what it means to be sorry for your sins?" She pantomimed tears and put her hand over her heart. I could feel myself relaxing. Lori could read. Lori could think. Lori understood abstract concepts. We read on in the lesson, the eraser of my pencil pointing the way, and Lori making muttering sounds.

When we came to the word "baptize" in our lesson, she let me know vigorously that she knew about baptism by pointing to the sanctuary where the baptism font is. Then she picked up a picture of parents holding a baby before their pastor, and she hugged and kissed it. I sensed her deep fondness for a baby.

We read together *why* John baptized those who repented and were sorry for their sins: that the water was a *picture* of washing away the people's dirty sins. Could Lori read and understand these words? She enthusiastically let me know she could. I had expected silence, but I got — not words exactly — but attempts at words and eloquent sounds of affirmation and gestures of sins being washed from her heart. She did this by pantomiming tears falling from her eyes down to her heart, and then gentle oval motions of cleansing over her heart.

We spent much of our lesson time on the story of Jesus coming to John to be baptized. I wrote to Lori that it was the part of the lesson which helps us understand *God.* Would Lori understand what I had written? We read the last two verses of the chapter: "And Jesus, when he was baptized, went up straightway out of the water: and, lo, the heavens were opened unto him, and he saw the Spirit of God descending like a dove, and lighting upon him: and lo a voice from heaven, saying, This is my beloved Son, in whom I am well pleased."

Lori said, "Oh," and gave me a look of quiet awe. I explained that the voice from heaven was God's voice and I asked on the chalkboard, "How many Gods do we have, Lori?"

She wrote, "one."

We read on in the lesson: "We have one God in three Persons — Father, Son, and Holy Spirit. Do you know that?"

She wrote, "No."

"The three Persons are in heaven, Lori, but once God sent His Son Jesus to the earth. He lived on the earth for thirty-three years."

Lori interrupted, picked up the chalk, and wrote, "Lori 20."

We caught the thread of the lesson again, and ended by stressing the simple truth that Jesus is God, and that He came to live on our earth for one reason: to wash away our sins by dying on the cross. His *blood* washed them away. Baptism is a picture of being washed clean of our sins by Jesus' blood.

I told her the last verse of the chapter would be our special verse for the week, and asked her to read it with her lips (I pointed to them) and with her throat (I pointed again). She tried to read it — not very clearly, for she never would speak clearly — with the effort of her whole body. We marked the verse in her Bible and I asked her to read it every night before she went to bed.

Lori glowed. She picked up her Bible, pressed the verse to her lips, and kissed it. Then she wrote on the board, "Lori love. Lori learn."

We spent the last few minutes of our time writing notes about our families, to get better acquainted.

"What a *nice* girl Lori is!" were my first words as I walked into the house that night. Lori impressed me not only with her receptivity, but with her *eagerness* to learn. She had looked at me intently. I could not yet be sure whether she liked the attention or was truly eager to learn the truths unfolded in the Scriptures. Not very much later, I knew it was the latter.

When Lori's Aunt Marcia asked me why Lori confided to her that Matthew 3:17 would always be her favorite verse in the Bible, I could not give her an answer. I thought she had been impressed — no, *awed* — by it, but it would be two years later before I had the full answer to that question.

* * * * * * * * * * * * * * * * * * *

In our second lesson, Lori learned how the devil tempted Jesus. She had never heard the history of the devil. I had anticipated this, and told her a brief history of the devil's fall. She read it intently and then showed me how it made her heart sink. Though she had not known the history of the devil, she *did* know the *work* of the devil. Very volubly, with words, gestures, and chalk on the communication board, she described the devil's work in some of the students at Kent Occupational High School. I did not know Lori's language well enough yet to understand everything she tried to tell me, and probably it was just as well. I was satisfied that she understood the power of evil.

The next part of the lesson was a stark contrast. Lori went on to read the circumstances of our Lord's temptation by the devil: "Jesus went forty days and forty nights without food. It was as long as a person can live without food." I wanted Lori to sense the weakened physical condition of Jesus just before His temptation.

I asked, "Lori, how do you think Jesus felt after forty days without food?"

She confidently picked up the pencil and wrote on the lesson, "chicken."

My puzzled look exasperated her. She grabbed the chalk and wrote, "chicken dinner — best dinner for Jesus," and she showed me by setting an elaborate imaginary table how she would serve that chicken dinner to Jesus. Lori's love and sympathy were always on the foreground, especially for her Jesus.

In the following weeks we emphasized the parables and the miracles of Jesus for Lori (and my other girls) as the concrete stories which help us understand the spiritual truths the Lord wants us to learn. Every lesson with Lori seemed special, but the lessons also fell into a routine. I handed her the four by six index card, pointed to her lips and throat, and she tried to read the prayer. We held hands and said, "Amen." After the first lesson, that was not enough. She left her chair and gave me a bear hug, and then kissed the words of the prayer.

As soon as these expressions of love were over, it seemed that she was suddenly composed and ready for the new lesson. Each week we had a review, with blanks to fill or multiple choice, or I asked a question such as, "What do you think?" She would pick up her pencil for her "test," as she called it, and with groans, sighs, and sounds she was not aware of, occasioned by her great concentration, would start working on the review sheet. Usually she prefaced it with a pantomime of studying hard, of finding the Bible passage and reading it, and often she handed me a neatly-written page with a favorite passage of the Bible copied on it.

If a question seemed especially simple to her, she looked sidewise at me, snapped her fingers, and said loudly, "Aha!" What she meant by this favorite expression, of course, was, "Ahead of you again!" If I wrinkled my nose ever so slightly to show that it was all in fun, she tickled me in my ribs.

Then she was immediately serious. We would start the new lesson, read it, explain some concepts on the chalkboard, and check the Bible for references. Often there were blanks in the lesson for Lori to fill, such as, "Do you think so?" or "What would you have done?" to see whether her thoughts were still on the lesson and whether she was understanding what she read.

Soon I discovered that the many visual aids were not necessary for Lori. She gave them a perfunctory glance, shoved them aside, and pointed to her head. That meant: "I understand. I don't need them. Shall we act as grown-ups?" I was learning!

Lori studied her worksheet noisily. She gasped, groaned, grunted, sighed, cheered, and oh-h-h-d and ah-h-h-d in amazement when she discovered a new truth, without ever knowing about all her noises. She was generous with her signs to demonstrate how well she understood what she was reading. In a certain way, she still read like a first-grader, with her whole body swaying. But her comprehension of words and ideas was growing far beyond that of a young child, and far beyond the level of comprehension her teachers at school had estimated.

Each lesson seemed to be a gradual awakening for Lori. Her spontaneous "oh," usually followed by a quick hug, told me she had grasped yet another precious truth. For me it was a revelation. She was much more advanced mentally and receptive spiritually than I could ever have dreamed. Not only could Lori understand the meanings of Jesus' parables and miracles, but she tried to tell me what they taught *her* before she read the explanation in her lesson. She had not known the truths of Scripture because no one had ever sat down and taught her. That first year of teaching Lori will always be a special year to recall. It was filled with what I came to think of as "Lori stories."

* * * * * * * * * * * * * * * * * *

Weddings intrigued Lori. When she saw that our next lesson was taken from John 2, and was about a wedding at Cana, she went into ecstasies about the weddings she had attended or served in as a flower girl; and I hoped I could make her understand the spiritual reality of Jesus' miracle at Cana when her thoughts were filled with bridal dresses and flowers. We read the story and learned how the family did not have enough wine, how this was not so strange, since wedding feasts often lasted several days in Bible times. Lori interrupted. I had learned her sign for that. I couldn't miss it! She gave a quick flick of her right hand, and then rested it right over the subject material. Taking the chalk, she wrote, "Lori like — Thanksgiving — Christmas — turkey," and she started a list of the guests she would invite to *her* feast. I mimicked her gesture of interruption, and we came back to the lesson, but not until she had chucked me under the chin.

She became serious again, and ready to learn. Following the lead of my pencil, she read the account of Jesus' instructions to the servants to fill the water pots to the brim — with *water.* She read that Jesus, by a wonder only He can do, because He is God, changed the water into wine.

I had an immediate response. She wrote, "Wine — Strong — you like?"

I shrugged my shoulders.

"You like?" she asked again.

"Only sometimes, Not very well."

"Beer!" she said, very plainly, and then "ble-a-a-h!" and graphically made herself a beer-belly.

I laughed and she rubbed my arm, to quiet me, I think. Next she pointed to the ring finger on my left hand, then to her hair, and said something that sounded like, "Vite like?"

I didn't understand.

She tried again. I still did not understand. "You stupid?" she wrote on the board.

"Yes," I answered.

Lori was persistent. She tried again. Pointing to my ring, she wrote, "Married?"

"Yes. . . ."

She caricatured my husband's stern face and upright posture, pointed to her hair, and wrote, "White?"

The light dawned. What Lori asked was, "Does white-haired husband like wine?"

"Yes, some wines," I wrote.

After that, her symbol for my husband was a quick touch to the ring finger, a tap on a lock of hair, and "Vite?"

We were quite far from Jesus' miracle at Cana. We still had to learn the most important part of the lesson: the meaning of what Jesus did. I told Lori (on the lesson sheet) that Jesus did not change water into wine only to help the family to serve their guests, but Jesus did this wonder because it was a *sign*. It had a *meaning*, a meaning for our hearts. Lori said, "Oh." She was understanding. Jesus *wanted* to work His first miracle at a wedding, because Jesus is the Bridegroom. Yes, Lori knew what a bridegroom is. Who is Jesus' bride? His church, His people. "You see, Lori," I wrote, "Jesus came down from heaven and lived on the earth with His bride for a few years, and He taught His bride with pictures and signs."

My deaf Lori knew all about pictures and signs.

"When Jesus changed the water into wine, He was making a *sign* of something. The wine that Jesus made at Cana was a picture of another wedding feast, when all His people, His bride, will join Him in heaven, to live with Him in joy and gladness forever. Jesus promised us that when we live with Him forever in heaven, no one will be sick, or sad, and no one will be deaf anymore."

Quietly, Lori picked up the chalk, and wrote, "I be very happy."

* * * * * * * * * * * * * * * * * *

Each Monday evening, Lori entered the hall of Hudsonville Church with a heavy step and a poker face, her usual way of entering a place where she would meet people, and stood quietly until the catechism class meeting in the room next to ours was dismissed. Suddenly, she was a vibrant Lori, meeting friends, going from one to another, making her too-loud noises, being shushed, and giggling. . . until I tapped her shoulder and said, "Time." Sometimes her footsteps to Room 3 were rather heavy and slow.

As soon as she was in the classroom, she was a pleasant Lori again, all ready to start the lesson. She started the habit of rubbing my arm affectionately, and then writing quick personal notes on the chalkboard, before I could get to the lesson. This led to a five-minute news time before class started. We wrote in fragments and incomplete sentences. Usually Lori wrote cheerfull little tidbits: "Fun basketball today — Terry likes Lori."

31

But when she was unhappy, no one needed to ask her how she felt. She showed it in every inch of her body. Though sympathetic to a dear, troubled, deaf girl, I usually discouraged her from spilling all her troubles to me before the lesson started. Often the lesson helped her. It seemed that the Lord spoke right to her problems through the lesson material, as He did this night when Lori came in very glum, and when we studied Luke 7, the story of Simon and the Woman.

We prayed our written prayer together, started the lesson, but it did not go as well as usual. In the first place, Simon, the host, was a Pharisee, and Lori knew what Pharisees were like. She hated them. She loathed them, and she scowled while reading the lesson. She learned that Simon invited Jesus to dinner, but when He came, Simon was impolite and rude. When he did not even give Jesus water to wash His dusty feet and when he gave Him no welcome, her fist came down hard on the paper. As I stroked the feisty little hand, she gave a wan semblance of a smile. We went on.

In order to make the situation come clear to Lori, I described, in words and diagram, that they ate reclining on couches, resting their heads on one hand. We both tried the position, but didn't do very well because we had no couches. Back to the lesson we went, and Lori read the explanation: "These were the olden days of long ago. People did not live as we do, and they did not have the nice things we have."

Instantly she picked up the chalk, and wrote, "No TV either."

In the next part of the lesson the woman entered. "She was not invited, Lori. She just came in, and the people at the feast were surprised and angry. Do you know why? She was a bad woman. Everyone there knew she lived a very sinful life. She came and stood at Jesus' feet.

"She came to Jesus' feet because she was so very sorry for all her sins. She cried and washed His feet with her tears and wiped them with her hair. Then she poured a sweet-smelling, expensive ointment over Jesus' feet."

I never got to the point of asking Lori why this woman came to Jesus with tears, for instead, a solemn Lori wrote on the board, "Bad today — Mad with Tracy — Very bad — Temper," and a motion of a swift punch, followed by "Sorry." That was why Lori had come in so glum!

We left the repentant woman for a while and wrote about repentant Lori. She did the writing: "Sorry to Tracy," with motions of hugs and kisses. Because it was so necessary that Lori be sorry not only to Tracy, but first of all to Jesus, I wrote, "Tell Jesus, too, Lori. Ask Him to take that sin away."

A somber Lori and I finished the lesson and had closing prayer. As I often did when I prepared her prayers, I had asked the Lord "to make us sorry for our sins, and to wash them all away in Jesus' blood." The Lord heard a very vocal response to our prayer that night. I could not understand everything Lori said, but I knew the Lord did.

It was time to dismiss. Lori held up the prayer card and made the motion of reading, and then put both hands at the side of her tilted head to indicate going to sleep. I nodded yes, that she might take the card and pray it again at home before she went to sleep, and gave her the card. She kissed it and she kissed me, and then wrote the word "Love," all the way around the chalkboard as a border, and then "Mrs. Hoeksema" inside her frame of love.

I motioned, "Why?"

She wrote, "Teach girls Bible."

I thought about it on the way home. Because Lori associated

me with the new joys of her salvation, and because she was so
happy, her outlet was to express love for the person who was
teaching her. And I was happy, too. Dear Lori had found re-
pentance and forgiveness.

* * * * * * * * * * * * * * * * * * *

So that Lori would understand the spiritual truths underlying
the stories in our lessons, whether they were parables or miracles,
I color-cued thoughts and special meanings in blue, and all
questions in red. I interspersed them through the lesson to keep
her alert. Nine o'clock in the evening was not prime lesson
time, and I wondered whether Lori always felt well. She seemed
sluggish at times.

Our next lesson, taken from Luke 5 and Mark 1, told the story
of two of Jesus' disciples, Peter and Andrew, fishing all night on
the Sea of Galilee and catching nothing. In the morning, after
Jesus had taught the people, He asked Peter to row his boat to
the deep part of the lake to fish. Although Peter did not feel
like it, he obeyed because *Jesus* told him to go, and he caught
so many fish the net broke.

34

Lori interrupted with an "Aha!" First we talked about some of Lori's fishing trips and then discussed the wonder of this great miracle, on our lesson sheet and on the chalkboard. Then came the meaning of this wonder, underlined in blue. Lori read: "The sea is a picture of the world of people. When Jesus' disciples threw their net into the sea, it was a picture of preaching the gospel — the good news — of Jesus to all people. Jesus called those disciples *by their names* to be fishers of men. That means they were to be preachers and to preach to men in Jesus' name."

There was utter silence. I bent my face down to hers, pointed to my head with the "understand?" gesture. She pushed me aside with her "I'm thinking" gesture. After a while she picked up the chalk and wrote, "Rev. Van Baren — Good man — Man of God — Fisherman-preacher, too — Love."

She had grasped it! Once more she made impatient motions at my enthusiasm. She was not finished. Tentatively, she wrote, "Call Lori's name, too?"

Now she was running ahead of me, for I had finished the lesson by telling her that Jesus does not call everyone to be *preachers,* but He calls *all* His children by their names. Lori sighed and drew a heart under her name. It was the start of her godly witness for the rest of her life.

Chapter 5

Lori Loves Church

In December I reported to our consistory, at their request, about the progress of the four girls I was teaching. I will quote the paragraphs which report specifically on Lori's progress. Although the reader has already learned some of the information in the letter, these paragraphs give a close-up picture of Lori, taken right on the scene.

In teaching Lori, I had to overcome more obstacles. We even have a unique way of opening with prayer. I write out a prayer and she gestures to let me know that she understands what we are praying, and at the end we both say "Amen" together. I write out her stories, first asking review questions from last week's lesson, and then telling the new story, interspersing the new story with questions such as, "What do you think. . . ?" to see whether she is following the line of the story. I color-cue her lessons, underlining all questions in red and boxing in the spiritual applications in blue. She often writes, "important" on the small portable chalkboard when we come to the blue boxes. That portable board, which I asked of the consistory, is my most valuable aid in teaching these children.

Lori responds with many gestures to show me she understands or does not understand; and from her responses to the review questions, which are almost always correct, I believe she understands the content and meaning of the stories. I am also teaching her how to use her Bible, to find passages and to read them in the context of the story. This she does with high enthusiasm and giggles of delight.

We are learning to communicate and as we learn to know one another better, I am convinced that Lori knows and can do far more than I had believed possible. Lori, along with the other girls, gives a clear and sincere spiritual response. We as members of God's church know that although a child may be impaired physically or mentally, the Spirit of God in her is not limited, for there are no limits to the blessings of God's Spirit. Yet I think that we tend to forget the work of the Spirit with our impaired children. But since I began teaching them, I cannot forget it, for the Holy Spirit and His work are always present with us. When we face our handicaps — and we do — we ask God's grace to make us know that He cares for us, *with* our handicaps and *because of* our handicaps. Lori gave a most precious comment on her problem when I wrote at the end of one lesson that in heaven no one will be sad or sick or deaf. I wrote, "In heaven, Lori, you will

will be able to hear." She wrote back, "I be very happy."

But handicapped teenagers do not want to study Bible lessons exclusively. My girls were looking forward eagerly to the Christmas holidays and all the exciting activities at this special time of the year. In a certain sense they had never lost their childish enthusiasm and naivete about presents and celebrations. Already during the month of November, when my four special girls met in the hall at church, coming and going from their lessons, they discussed getting together as a group, and I encouraged them. I often felt sad when I saw them after services or at special events at church, standing apart, rather alone. They did not quite fit with the other young people, who talked of cars and dates and jobs. If these girls could get together by themselves, in friendship and for fun, wouldn't they have a great time?

We decided to have a craft party, where we would make gifts for our parents, on a Saturday afternoon early in December in Room 3 at Hudsonville Church. The four girls were invited, along with Marcia, a special friend of Betty. Betty had told her about our craft party and she was very eager to join us; and from then on, Marcia always joined us for crafts.

Our daughter Eunice offered to help with the first craft party. She came with a choice of planters from her cold ceramics business. Each girl chose the cold ceramic planter she wanted. Then Eunice showed them how to paint and wax the planters. Because the process required steady hands and concentration, it was a bold venture for a craft party, but all the girls insisted they were ready for the challenge.

On Saturday afternoon everyone came dressed in old clothes and we covered the table with thick layers of newspapers. With Eunice's help, each started painting the planter of her choice. At first there was silence, tongues twisted in concentration, with an occasional "whoops!" when globs of paint landed in the wrong places.

Eunice noticed that Lori was not following instructions. She bent over her to show her the proper technique, but Lori pushed her aside, grabbed her brush, and did it her own way. Quick as a flash, Glenda, more of a helper than handicapped, stood in front of Lori, put her finger in her face, scolded her, and said, "You obey! You don't know it all!"

Lori's face told us that she had successfully read Glenda's lips. She put down her brush and looked around. All the girls were frowning at her. She couldn't take *that*! Turning, she smiled (in as far as Lori could smile) at Eunice, handed her the brush, and learned how to do it the right way. Betty was already writing on the board, "Now you're nice, Lori."

From that afternoon on, Eunice and Lori were fast friends. And when we voted whose planter was the best, everyone agreed it was Lori's. Then came the flurry of wrapping, making cards, and cleaning up. Lori was meticulous when it came to leaving things as we had found them. When I went to check the sink in the girls' room, I found Lori already there, scrubbing it. When she finished, she took my hand, pulled me back to Room 3, picked up the chalk, and wrote, "Hudsonville Church — God's house — Holy — tomorrow Sunday — not to make dirty Sat. — Lori clean," with motions of shock as to how the congregation would react if they saw our mess.

I had promised to take Lori home. During the first part of our ride, we had a little conversation about the success of our afternoon, but soon Lori's eyes were closing. I thought she may have tired because of her diabetes. She often tired quickly, more quickly than I would expect from a girl of her robust build. But I did not know why.

In three short months, Lori had taken a large place in my life. Even at the special Christmas gathering for the adult societies in our congregation which we attended, I could not forget my Lori. This is what happened: at refreshment time, my husband and I were standing in one of the long lines. Lori's paternal grand-father was in another line, waiting for his refreshments. He motioned to me and called me over. I did not know this tall, white-haired, rather distinguished-looking man very well. In fact, I stood a bit in awe of him. He seemed somewhat austere. He didn't smile at me as I walked over, but asked, "What have you been doing to Lori?"

My heart sank. Was something wrong?

"Mr. Holstege, I'm sure you know that I have been trying to teach her Bible lessons."

"Mrs. Hoeksema, we can't help but know it," he said, as he came forward and gave me a hearty handshake. "We can't believe the remarkable change that has come over Lori since you taught her. She's different. Don't tell me you haven't noticed."

"How could I? I didn't even know Lori before I started teaching her this fall."

He smiled then, and said, "Whatever you're doing, keep it up. Don't stop teaching her. She's a different girl."

"Different how?"

"Well, it's rather hard to say, but we see it. She's more quiet inside, maybe. More satisfied. A more spiritual girl. Seems as if she had a spiritual awakening."

I thanked the kindly old gentleman for the encouragement, and I did not think he was so somber, after all.

* * * * * * * * * * * * * * * * * *

After Christmas break our lessons seemed easier in a way. We had learned how to communicate more satisfactorily, and Lori

40

had begun to understand the truths and the meanings of the gospel of salvation. In the limited time we had for our Bible lessons, she was a avid learner. She gave the lesson her intense concentration with her customary sighs and sounds. It was as if she was trying hard to make up for lost time, the time when she was younger and did not have the opportunity to learn these precious truths. I had begun to teach her how to use her Bible. We faced the question of which version we would use. Would the King James Version be understandable and suitable for a handicapped girl? For Lori? I knew her poetic soul would love it, but would she understand? Then I remembered my first graders of years back. If they could understand, Lori certainly could.

A little later, after we had been reading from our Bibles for some weeks, she told me, "Like words in Holy Bible — God — Holy — Thee — Thou." Her broken sentence told me that she felt the reverence, the *difference* of Scripture, different words and a different tone from the words and tone of daily conversations and of her textbooks.

We started learning how to use our Bibles by turning to the gospel narratives, because they told the story of Jesus' life on earth; and that was our lesson material. Lori had her own choices of some of the verses we read, and put markers in the pages. Soon her Bible was bulging with slips of paper. It was time for her to find these texts on her own, and not rely on markers. We practiced finding one of my favorite texts, John 10:11. Lori had not realized that she must look for the word *John* first. After she found the book, I pointed to the 10, and she traveled to chapter 10; and then I encouraged the plodding finger to go to verse 11, a tedious process. I asked her to read the verse while the eraser of my pencil led the way. I pointed to her lips and throat, and she read the verse aloud: "I am the good shepherd: the good shepherd giveth his life for the sheep."

She thought for a moment, and wrote on the chalkboard,

"Shepherd = Jesus," and drew a cross next to it, poked me, pointed to her head in a gesture of "I understand," and then kissed the text. We had not yet formally studied our Lord's suffering and death, but we could not progress very far in our lessons without looking ahead to the death of our Savior, and what it means for us. Lori had much more to learn, but she was grasping the basic concepts of faith in her Lord Jesus.

The next week she came to class with the passage about the Good Shepherd neatly copied. She put her hands together on the side of her head to show bed-time, and told me she had read it every night. On the board she wrote "Mon — Tue — Wed. . ." all the days of the week in abbreviated form.

* * * * * * * * * * * * * * * * * * * *

Now that Lori had a fairly good start in her Bible lessons, I started laying plans to correct the great problem in her life: the way she attended church. Crassly put, she sat in church like "a bump on a log." The lesson for our next Monday evening session would probably give me the opening I needed.

On that Monday evening, we followed Jesus and His disciples as they walked through the cornfields on the sabbath day. It was like our Sunday, I told Lori. They were picking and eating corn, and the Pharisees ("ble-a-a-h!" was Lori's reaction), who were always close at hand, scolded them for it. When Lori read on that Jesus taught His disciples that He did not come to make all kinds of rules: "Do this" and "Don't do that" on His day, her head was nodding in hearty agreement. She herself did not like rules very well. But when we learned that Jesus said that God gives us our Sunday to *use* — to serve Him and worship Him on His day — she sank back into her chair, deflated.

"Lori not like church," went on the board. "Only baptism — babies," and like a whipped puppy she looked at me for under-standing.

Under her plaintive confession, imitating her telegraphic style, I wrote, "Not so bad, Lori. I would not like to go to church if I were a deaf girl — could not hear — didn't know what was happening — I don't blame you."

Almost before I was finished, I was smothered with a powerful hug, and it was my turn to beg for mercy. After some giggling, I told her I had a secret plan.

"Tell," she begged on the chalkboard.

"To make your Sundays happy in the Lord's work."

Once more she sank back and was quiet as the implications of what I had written sank in. I could see that she was having mixed feelings about it.

That week I went to talk with Pastor Van Baren ("good man:" now I was taking over Lori's way of thinking) and bemoaned the fact that Lori had always sat in a vacuum during the most important hours of the week. I told him I did not blame her for hating something she should have loved the most: worshipping her Lord. It need not be that way, for Lori had demonstrated unmistakably that she was not only *able* to worship, but *eager.* All I needed was the approval of my plans and his cooperation. As an added incentive for his cooperation, I added that he had not forgotten at whose suggestion I was "volunteered" for this work, had he? In his quiet way, Pastor Van Baren laughed at my way of putting it, and was agreeable to the plans. No, he was excited and he was heartily willing to help me all he could.

Next I had a conference with Lori's father, and he agreed to cooperate with the plan. He realized it was coming late in her life, and urged me to start very soon. I did.

Our next lesson was not a regular Bible lesson, but was titled "Something Special," and was a set of detailed plans.

"Lori," the lesson began, "would you like to take part in every bit of the church service on Sunday and understand it, so that you can be busy with the Lord's work with all the rest of God's people?"

The enthusiasm of her response brought tears, first to me, and then to her. She stood up, wound her arms around me, saying, far too loudly, "Lori like! Lori like!" Those two words, along with her "Oho's," told just how much her dear soul longed for participation in the worship services. She *wanted* to understand, to participate, to be a conscious part of the body of Christ, but until now her profound deafness had prevented it. No one, for her first nineteen years, had tried to help her participate fully in church services. Tonight we were to take the first step to correct that negligence. Both of us were unsure of ourselves but more than eager to try.

We pored over the plans, which included the necessity of her sitting next to me in the pew, so that I could help her during the service. When we came to this part of the plans, Lori flicked her hand for her interruption signal, pointed to my wedding ring, and asked "Vite?" It always came out more "Vite" than "White." Yes, white-haired husband would be with us, too.

The next Sunday morning as we came into the narthex, we met an eager Lori, ready to sit with us, with an important-looking ring-bound notebook under her arm. The first question she asked, by gesture, was, "Do I look all right?" She did. She was meticulous about her personal appearance.

Lori beamed. She walked tall this morning. I had some quiet reservations: was she thrilled because of all the attention and because of the novelty of sitting with us — which was reasonable, to a degree — or was it truly from a deep desire to worship with us?

We three were ushered in, and Lori nodded and smiled to all her friends and then commented to me about announcements on the bulletin that caught her eye, and generally acted like a proud princess.

The service started with silent prayer. After some coaching, Lori had written on the chalkboard the previous Monday evening what she would pray for during the silent prayer:

"Rev. Van Baren — preach — bless —
Lori — learn — love Bible
Sing good"

Lori had never sung in church. On Monday evening we had studied the structure of notes, what long and short ones, high and low ones looked like. But Lori said not to worry. Joe, her friend at school, played a horn, and he showed her how long and short notes looked. He must have taught her more, for Lori tapped out a schmaltzy rhythm.

During our lesson, I also extracted a promise from her that she would use her lips and her voice when we sang. She was lazy about opening her mouth and trying to vocalize; and it was understandable, because of her impaired muscles on one side of her throat. But her voice would not develop with disuse, and Lori understood that, too.

The congregation stood for the doxology. My four by six index card, with the doxology typed on it, was ready. What a thrill we had: Lori followed the eraser of my pencil as I tapped the rhythm, and for the first time in her life, she sang, "Praise God, from Whom all blessings flow. . . " with the congregation. I know. I heard her voice.

For the salutation and the blessing, I turned the card over, and we read these words, while the rest of the congregation listened to the pastor's words: "Our help is in the name of Jehovah Who made heaven and earth. Beloved in the Lord Jesus Christ: Grace, mercy, and peace be unto you from God the Father and from Jesus Christ our Lord, through the operation of the Holy Spirit. Amen."

Before the service started, I had asked Lori to find the numbers of the songs we were to sing. It was good practice for her, and she followed the listing on the board in the front of the auditorium and put markers in her Psalter. It would help us with the busyness of the mechanics of the service. We sang together, although she let me know that it bothered her that "Vite" had to sing alone. I tapped the rhythm and she voiced the words. It was evident that Lori had been a lazy church-goer, and was not accustomed to intensive participation. When she lagged or her attention wandered, a pencil tap on her arm brought her back, and she diligently tried to follow again. Her whole body swayed with the effort, and at the end of the first song, she tilted her head for my smile of approval.

Had we not been so occupied with the mechancis of participating and with Lori's newly-found happiness, we might have been conscious of what was going on around us. It was not until after the service that the friends and relatives who came up to us said they were so touched when they saw Lori singing the Lord's praises in the communion of saints for the first time, that they choked up, the tears flowed, and the handkerchiefs came out.

Lori and I were so busy we did not notice. Lori was not accustomed to this fast pace in church. Another index card was already in front of her, for the minister had already started to read the law, and we were not ready. We caught up and she followed my pencil as she did in class, with an "oh" of discovery and a look at me when something new struck her, forgetting that her pastor had kept on reading, and we had lost some words. In the stillness of the church service, I realized just how noisy her reading and reactions were, and although I hated to do it, I asked her to read more quietly. I motioned that she must not disturb others.

46

For the congregational prayer, I had typed a special prayer for Lori. She had very little instruction in either the form or content of prayer. Lori and I both thought it would be a good idea for me to make prayers with different themes, and in that way she would learn the art of prayer. I told her that the Bible would be our textbook on prayer, and the Bible never runs out of things to teach us about prayer. In this first prayer, besides praying for her needs and the needs of the congregation, Lori's prayer centered on the theme of Jesus as the Good Shepherd. This theme was becoming one of her favorites, and she had already asked me for passages on the Shepherd and His sheep to copy from her Bible. In this first prayer she read, in part:

> Psalm 23 tells us, "The Lord is my Shepherd." That is a wonderful picture. A shepherd takes care of his sheep and loves his sheep and will not let a wild animal eat his sheep. And the Bible tells us that *we* are Thy sheep. I am one of Thy sheep, too. Thou, God, callest all Thy people Thy sheep. We need Thee every day. We need our God to give us our food, our health, and to take care of us when we go to school. It is a great wonder, O Lord, that Thou dost take care of all Thy people at the same time. The Bible says that our Shepherd leads us in green pastures. We know that those green pastures are Thy Holy Word, the Bible. Just as sheep eat grass, we eat Thy Word, not with our mouths, but with our hearts. We could not live without the food of Thy Word.

In the middle of our prayer, she could not resist poking me and sharing her happiness in her prayer. She had instructions to read the prayer twice, carefully, then think for a while, and on the blank lines below to write a prayer of her own. Her first prayer was a very simple one, asking God to bless us in church.

She was amazed when I poked her and told her the prayer was over, and it was time for the offering. Then came a song again. The logistics of following the order of worship made for a very busy service.

Pastor Van Baren had given me a short summary of the divisions of his sermon. I added to it, asking some questions and leaving blanks for her answers. Lori copied proof texts, which she could now find by herself, and she went to work, with her paper on a sturdy clip-board; and was soon absorbed in her "sermon." She took a few breathers to limber her fingers, rub my arm, put her face in front of mine, and sigh in contentment.

Near the end of the service, I wrote one word on her paper: "Tired?" She nodded, but her face looked as if she was happy that she was tired. We finished the service with Lori participating in the song and doxology.

It had been a busy time, and although I had rubbed her arm a few times to tell her that her participation was top-notch, I was a little uneasy. In order to keep her busy, we had to have limited communications during the service. And dear Lori's enthusiasm was so great, it was hard to keep her silent. She *would* make noise! As we walked out of church, I was ready to make an apology of sorts to the friends who sat behind us. They must have read my thoughts on my face, because they started first: "Don't shush her!" And one warm, motherly woman told us, "It was the best service I've ever attended, even though I wiped my eyes when she sang."

Others came up to me: "Don't worry about disturbing. Lori taught us something this morning about the joys of participating in worship. We will never take it for granted again."

They said they were thrilled that Lori could participate and understand. They said they just loved it. So did Lori: and surrounded by her friends, she displayed her "sermon."

* * * * * * * * * * * * * * * * * * * *

Lori liked Pastor Van Baren. He was a "good man," but she did not get close to him. My husband experienced the same kind of treatment. Because he and I belonged together, he had to come along and sit with us in church. She was friendly and reserved toward him, and always spoke of him as "Vite." One Sunday

48

evening he had to preach for us while Pastor Van Baren was supplying a pulpit elsewhere. Earlier in the week he had given me his sermon outline, and I made a detailed resume, in simple language, with blanks to fill in from Bible texts, and words to underline.

That evening Lori was especially bubbly in church. I did not know whether it was because she had a more detailed sermon or whether she identified with the preacher. Probably it was a bit of both. On the other hand, excitement and intense concentration tired Lori rather quickly. And I could not forget the impact her new life with the Lord was making on her. She was happy — no, jubilant! But she was learning so much so fast. I must be careful not to overwhelm her. Besides, Lori was a severe diabetic. I had not seen any adverse reactions as yet, but I knew I wanted to be gentle and careful with this dear girl.

I started the practice of writing now and then on her sermon paper, "Take a break." During this service, her subdued sighs and gasps were almost constant. She was working hard tonight, when she came to, "Take a break." She stretched, looked around a bit, and then picked the Psalter out of the rack. She stopped at a versification of Psalm 116:
    I love the Lord, the fount of life and grace;
    He hears my voice, my cry and supplication,
    Inclines His ear, gives strength and consolation;
    In life, in death, my heart will seek His face.

Laboriously she lipped the words, big ones and all, and in a loud whisper, said, "Oh, nice," pointed to her heart, and hugged the Psalter. How could I repress such an irrepressible girl? I wondered, though, why this particular stanza captured her. I still do. She turned to it repeatedly during later services.

I called her back to her unfinished sermon work, and she got busy. Then the sermon was over, and Lori was still absorbed "in Lord's work," as she called it. I poked her and made the "all finished" sign. She looked up with an astonished look on her face, and said, far too loudly, "Huh?" and then realized her blunder and clapped her hand over her mouth. What else could we do but giggle? She didn't want to pay attention to the closing song. She kept insisting that "Vite" was "too short."

After that incident, I never again worried about her disturbing the quiet decorum of our services, when Lori was so busy doing the "Lord's work." Besides, we knew that everyone was pulling for Lori.

That was not the end of the matter. After the service, she marched boldly to my husband, something she had never done before, and motioned, "Too short." He had used every minute of the service, without going overtime. He motioned back, "Too long." She would not be convinced, and I heard repeatedly afterwards that "Vite was too short." Knowing Lori better now, I think it was tongue-in-cheek. I think she was beginning to realize that time went by fast when she was busy with the Lord's work. Although Lori smiled her half-smile sweetly and nonchalantly when her friends encouraged her, she seemed to know what they were seeing: a changed Lori, who was fast becoming the pet of the congregation.

* * * * * * * * * * * * * * * * * * *

For several weeks in the beginning of the year 1983, we studied Jesus' miracles of healing. Lori read the description of leprosy in her lesson one Monday evening: "Leprosy was a terrible sickness. First, small sores came on a person's hands or eye-lids. Then his hair and skin turned white. Open sores made his body rot away. Sometimes the sickness made him lose his mind, too. It was a *living death*. Can you understand why, Lori. . . ?"

She looked up at me and nodded her head. We read in our lesson that such a leper came to Jesus, and said to Him, "If thou wilt, thou canst make me clean." Lori read it from her Bible in Mark 1:40, which she found by herself.

Back to the lesson sheet, we read, "The leper had _____.
Confidently, she filled in *faith.* We read on: "Jesus touched him
and said, 'I will; be thou clean.' Then Jesus said something surprising. He told the man, 'See thou say nothing to any man.'
He was telling this man not to tell anyone about this great
wonder! Why not?"

Lori studied the words in her Bible again, and shook her head.

I took my hand away from the answer I was covering on the
lesson sheet, and she read, "Because Jesus did not want the
people, *and us,* to think that Jesus was just a doctor who healed
people's bodies, and nothing more."

She followed the eraser of my pencil as we went on: "Jesus
wanted the leper to know that when He healed that poor man's
body, it was a picture of healing his soul, which was filled with
the living death of sin."

Lori touched her heart and shook her head sadly.

We went on: "Jesus felt sorry for the man and healed his body
from leprosy and his soul from sin. Do you know what Jesus
gave to that man? *Salvation.*"

She picked up the chalk and wrote, "to Lori, too." She, too,
knew the salvation her Lord had given *her.*

The facets of Lori's character fascinated me. She could be so
serious and intent on catching up with all the Bible knowledge
she had missed in her earlier years, but at the same time was
always ready for a clever little prank. I knew it, but usually was
taken in by it. The week after we had studied the story of Jesus
raising the daughter of Jairus from the dead, I gave this review
question on her worksheet: "Jesus raised Jairus' daughter from
the _____." She crossed out the *the* and wrote *sleeping*
on the blank, and looked at me with an innocent, straight face.
On the chalkboard, I asked, "She did not die?"

She pointed to her answer, and then reached for her Bible, with the passage already marked at Luke 8, verse 52. With exaggerated solemnity she motioned me to read it: "Weep not; she is not dead, but sleepeth." Laughing boisterously, she shook my shoulders, then calmed herself again as she wrote, "Lori knows." She also let me know, by putting her hands under her cheek and ticking off five fingers, that she had read the passage five nights before going to sleep.

"And that is when you dreamed up your trick," I teased, on the chalkboard. Her reply was a funny pantomime, which told me she understood the double meaning of my retaliation.

The story of Jesus stilling the tempest charmed Lori. I showed her some pictures of violent storms at sea, and described the wild fury of the Sea of Galilee. She read that Jesus was peacefully sleeping through the storm, but the disciples were afraid. They could not manage the boat because the waves were filling it with water. I asked Lori to read from her Bible the question they asked Jesus, and she read, "Master, carest thou not that we perish?"

She nodded when I told her the disciples were sure they would all drown. Then I asked her to read the three words Jesus spoke after they awakened Him, and she read, "Peace, be still."

Back to the lesson sheet, Lori read that "after Jesus' words of power made the sea calm, His disciples were still afraid, for they knew that the Almighty God was there in the ship with them, and they were afraid of His holiness and His power so great that the wind and sea obeyed Him."

Then: "Lori, if you were there, would you be afraid, knowing that Jesus was in the boat with you?"

She spread her hands in an "I don't know" motion. I told her to think. After a few false starts, she reached for the chalk, and slowly wrote:

52

Jesus is God
God is love
Lori not afraid

* * * * * * * * * * * * * * * * * * *

Naturally, Lori loved the story of Jesus healing the deaf man with an impediment in his speech, because it was her own story. She began reading on her lesson sheet: "Then a deaf man stood before Jesus. He could not speak because he had never heard anyone speak. . . ."

Lori interrupted in mid-sentence and wrote, "Lori not hear either."

". . . and because his tongue was tied in his mouth and he could not use it to make words."

Rather wistfully she picked up the chalk again and wrote, "Lori— many doctors — bad," and pointed to the crooked side of her mouth.

We read on: "Jesus took the man away from the crowds of people, by himself, because all his life he had to live in a world by himself."

We stopped again and she nodded her head and pointed to herself. She knew what it was to live in a world by herself. I thought she was going to cry, but she motioned to go on. She loved the next part, the part where Jesus used the words, "Eph-pha-tha," which were easy to lip-read. We practiced the words. And then Lori learned that Jesus said "Eph-pha-tha" to the man's ears and mouth because it meant "Be opened:" and they were opened. The man heard and he spoke.

We read how Jesus told the man not to tell anyone about the wonder, but now that he could talk, the man *could not* keep still.

"Lori not" went on the chalkboard, which I took to mean that she would not keep still, either!

We finished by trying to understand what Jesus' wonder meant: that it is only Jesus Who can open the ears of His people so they can hear His voice, and only Jesus Who can open the mouths of His people so they can praise Him.

It was quiet in Room 3. I sensed she was thinking, getting ready to communicate.

"Hear Jesus now," she wrote, and pointed to her heart; and then "Praise in church now."

She did not want me to question or comment. She was still pondering something. Soon it came on the board: "Not deaf in heaven — all better — angels," and pantomimed a choir and playing a trumpet.

I did not have a thing to add. Her attitude that evening breathed a quiet acceptance of her handicap and a looking forward to a perfect life without any defect, with Jesus and the angels.

* * * * * * * * * * * * * * * * * * *

In many ways, Lori acted like a typical teenager, always gravitating toward the favorites among her friends, the soft-natured girls, and boys, too, who had a true interest in her. I developed a leniency about starting class exactly at nine. We often started a bit late. One night when it was time for class to start, she held back and motioned me over. With signs and sounds, she asked me to go to the girls' room with her to see something Tammy had — I think it was a bracelet. I hesitated. It was more than time to start. She put her face in front of mine, put an arm around my shoulder, and I gave in. I put my arm over her shoulder, and off we rushed to the girls' room, and soon we were rushing back to pick up Lori's books. In the hall, near the door of Pastor Van Baren's classroom, stood a teenager of about sixteen, a former pupil of mine, a rather reticent boy who did not always communicate well, and who did not pay much attention to his former teacher now that first grade was far behind him. While Lori picked up her books, he sidled over to me, and said, a bit self-consciously, "You really love that girl, don't you! I can see why. She sure is a nice kid!" and he disappeared into his classroom. Lori had captured one more heart!

One of Lori's favorite people was Tammy. Physically, Tammy was everything that Lori was not: thin, lithe, coordinated, even-featured. Inside, Tammy was sympathetic, sweet, and loving, a true companion for Lori's personality. Tammy took time out from the chit-chat with her teenage friends to talk with Lori, and she made a staunch, life-long friend.

Lori and Tammy exchanged notes and cards on special occasions for several years. Lori loved to receive and share her notes, such as this one, from her friend. It shows Lori's near-normal and easy relationships with her teenage friends.

Dear Lori,

How are you doing? I haven't seen you in such a long time!! I went to Byron Church this past Sunday but you weren't there. I saw Debbie and Randy and I looked in the nursery, but didn't see you. Next time I go to your church I'll call your house and tell Debbie. Then if I see you there maybe I'll sit by you. How do you like going to your newly organized church? Quite a few families from Hudsonville have gone to Byron Church. So what have you been doing lately? Are you going to school yet? Are you working anywhere? How is your dog doing? Aren't you glad Christmas is coming? I love Christmas time. All the lights are so pretty. I saw some Christmas lights this past week!! It's kind of early to put out Christmas lights yet but it still looks very pretty. Well, take good care of yourself and maybe I'll see you at Byron Church and at catechism next week Monday night. I'll be looking for you! See ya soon!

Love, Your *Friend,*
Tammy

P.S. Write me a letter sometime and if you give it to Randy, maybe he can give it to me at school.

* * * * * * * * * * * * * * * * * * *

Toward the end of our first season of lessons, we studied Jesus'
suffering and death. We worked hard to finish, so Lori would
have an overview of what Jesus suffered to save her. It was the
evening for the lesson on the Lord's Supper. Lori had already
learned about the feast of the passover, and what it meant.
Using the setting of the upper room, I wrote, "Jesus gave His
disciples — and us — another kind of feast. It is called the Lord's
Supper. He took a piece of bread, gave thanks to God, and then
broke the bread and told each of His disciples to eat a piece of
the bread. It was a picture of Jesus' body being broken for their
sins and for our sins. Next Jesus poured wine into a cup and told
the disciples to drink the wine. It was a picture of Jesus' blood
which He poured out for their sins and for our sins. In our
churches today we still remember Jesus' body and blood with
the bread and the wine of the Lord's Supper, don't we?"

Lori read it, thought for a moment, and then stood up, grasped
my hand, and led me out of the room. Was it a sudden bathroom
emergency? No, she hurried me through the narthex to the back
of the sanctuary, as she had done once earlier this year when we
looked at the baptism font; and there we stood in the chilly darkness while she vigorously pointed out to me the placement of the
table for the bread and wine during communion services, meanwhile making motions of eating and drinking. I didn't know why
we were standing here. But by making motions of eating and
drinking and then pointing to her head and shaking it, and
making negative sounds, and moving her arms up and down in
wide sweeps, which were her motions for frustration and disgust,
a distraught Lori made me understand that she had seen the
sacrament often, but never knew the meaning of it. I was too
stunned to react, and we were both shivering. Slowly I coaxed
her back to the classroom, while she was either complaining or
explaining too loudly and utterly unintelligibly her feelings of
ignorance and disappointment with her new discovery.

It was the only time Pastor Van Baren opened his classroom door

56

to see whether we needed help. I shook my head and he retreated; and an upset teacher and pupil re-entered the classroom.

I was upset because a twenty-year-old girl had seen the outward signs and seals of her salvation all her life and had never understood them. No one had told her what they meant. How could I help her now?

Maybe the positive approach would be best. I wrote, "Be glad that you know now, Lori. Thank the Lord."

But Lori was not in that frame of mind. At first I thought she was not paying attention and was engrossed in her own thoughts as she kept up a steady series of "um-m-ms."

She erased my words and wrote her own: "Lori love Jesus — take Lord's Supper."

We spent the rest of our lesson time talking together on the chalkboard. We talked about Lori's regrets for having been "in the dark" all these years, and how we could not change what was past. She only sighed about it. It was not what she wanted to hear.

So I took a plunge: "I think the Lord wants you to learn some more truths before you take Lord's Supper, Lori. If you promise to study hard, I promise to get you ready for Lord's Supper. Not right away. First you must learn more in your head and in your heart."

Lori nodded somberly as we finished our lesson. But I knew that she would not let me forget my promise.

After the lesson was over and I had time to reflect on my spur-of-the-moment decision, I was rather amazed that I had made the promise. I had consulted no one. Before I could keep my promise, I would need advice, conferences with her parents, and with our pastor and council. But I was not sorry nor conscience-stricken that I had made the promise. When I asked myself why not, I had the answer: I *knew* that Lori was able not only mentally and spiritually to make a good confession, but that she was intensely eager to confess her faith.

We finished our lessons for the season in May, with the story of the resurrection of our Lord.

Chapter 6

Lori's Summer of '83

The celebration at the end of our first season of lessons was another happy get-together for a craft party. The girls wanted a Saturday afternoon get-together in early May to make Mother's Day gifts. At Lori's last lesson, when I wrote on the board that I would pick her up at 1:30 p.m. for the craft party, she cocked her head and wrote, "Eunice?" Yes, Eunice would help. We planned to try cold ceramics once more: this time we would do animals, and the girls chose cats or dogs sitting or lying in various positions.

On Saturday, when Eunice walked into our newspaper-cluttered room, she received a tremendous welcome, with "aha's" and bear hugs. Now we knew without a doubt that Eunice was accepted.

Craft parties with five handicapped girls do not always run smoothly, especially when Lori is the pet and everyone wants to help her and be her friend. Betty said she was jealous because I could communicate with Lori. Why couldn't Lori understand *her*? May she try to explain the next step to Lori? Betty tried. But she tried too hard. Lori sighed and wrote, "Pest." Betty was crushed and angry and stomped back to her ceramics. I wrote on the board, "Nice pest," and Betty jumped up and wrote, "I love you, Lori." Lori put down her brush and went over and hugged Betty, while I tried to explain that we all love her so much, we almost fight to help her. Could she accept a little help from all of us? She swallowed and accepted the situation, sort of, but her actions told us that she wanted Glenda and Eunice as helpers.

* * * * * * * * * * * * * * * * * *

Lori's parents and I decided to make use of all available time to teach her, and we arranged to have classes in my office at home during the summer months. The arrangement came at my suggestion. She was so hungry for Biblical truths, so ignorant of Bible history, and had such a long way to go! Besides, I could not bear the thought of not seeing Lori regularly and watching her blossom; and, yes, selfishly perhaps, I could not miss the enjoyment of the company of that dear girl.

During our first season of lessons, we had gone through some sad times together. Lori mirrored her feelings by her walk, her posture, and her expressive face. Often when she first walked into the classroom, I knew I need not ask if she was sad, and I set about to cheer her. The reason for her inner turmoil was that in the fall of 1982 her father and mother had separated, and Lori was struggling with the necessary adjustments in her life. Now her mother lived in an apartment, and Lori spent time at two homes. Her lessons cheered her when she was dejected. Because we were studying God's Word, He spoke to both of us, no matter what passage we studied, and Lori often wrote on the chalkboard, "Feel better now."

She was also very eager for summer sessions. We had decided to start at the beginning of the Old Testament. Lori told me she did not know very much about it.

The first time we met in my office, as I was preparing to start our first lesson on creation, Lori flicked her hand to interrupt. She looked at me with a poker face, which meant she had some scheme in mind. "Summer now," she wrote on the portable chalkboard we had moved from Room 3 for the summer. "Not so busy now."

I nodded agreement and waited.

"Eunice — not busy?"

I shrugged. Eunice had two very active young sons.

Lori persisted, made her not-so-far-away gesture, and said a word

60

that sounded like "Grandville." I interpreted her next motion as running her hand over something smooth. Then she simulated putting on a dress. Either she was vague or I was dense.

She slapped the desk, laughed at me, and used the chalk. "New dress — Sunday," and she made the motion of two swings of her hand for faraway Hudsonville and then peaked her hand for the roof of a church. I got that part.

Next came: "Eunice make? — Grandville Fabric — mother pay," and she made gestures of me using the telephone and asking her mother; and then of telephoning Eunice and getting her to cooperate. She did it by pointing in the exact directions of her mother's apartment and Eunice's home. Her sense of geographical relationships never failed her.

Now the whole secret scheme was out. What could I do but write, "I will work on it?" First came her loud "aha!" and then she tickled me, chucked me under the chin, and squeezed me. Lori would never need a course on how to win friends and influence people. It was useless for me to urge caution; I could only hope Eunice would do it for her.

She would. Lori's mom would pay for the fabric. At our next lesson we made plans. She thought that "Wed." would be a good day, and father had promised money for some ice cream afterward.

Jonathan, almost five, and David, almost three, Eunice's two sons, came along that Wednesday afternoon. At the store, first came the ritual of looking at pattern books. It was like a circus as she tried to get everyone's opinions at once. The books exchanged hands and the boys were full of suggestions. Lori had very definite dislikes. After we heard "Na-a-a-h" several times, we began to know her taste. When the choices were narrowed down to a few favorites, and Eunice and I were showing her what would be best, she turned to Jonathan. It came out

61

"Yonntun," and he came over and studied the pattern we would probably choose. We were laughing, too, when Lori poked fun of some of the totally unsuitable patterns. A gentle voice behind us said, "This must be a very special girl."

It was one of the clerks. "She is. Very special," Jonathan told her.

"She can't hear, but she understands us," young David volunteered.

I turned around to smile at the clerk, and discovered a small group of customers enjoying the fun with us. Jonathan paid no attention to them. "This is *perfect*, Lori," he said, and the matter was settled. Now for the fabric. While we looked, Lori held Jonathan's hand. Being a young boy, he was an explorer, but if he wandered away, she would simply command, "Yonntun, come," and they would stroll through the bolts of fabric hand-in-hand again.

We found the perfect fabric: soft reds and pinks on an eggshell background. Eunice and I discussed yardage and accessories, and Lori and Jonathan disappeared. We found them shortly, both sitting on the floor in front of a low rack of lace. They had already chosen the proper lace edging for the new dress.

Clerks and customers were still smiling when at last the time came to pay the bill.

"Is she a relative?" a clerk asked.

"No, but we love her," David answered, and then looked around amazed when everyone laughed. To David, love and happiness merged when we were with Lori. It isn't everyone who has such a happy time choosing fabric and lace, and then gets to have ice cream afterwards.

Almost more exciting for Lori were the fittings at Eunice's

house, the exploring of her refrigerator, and the going home with samples of baked goods for all the family. She wore the dress proudly that summer.

* * * * * * * * * * * * * * * * * * *

In the summer of 1983 I was finishing the manuscript of my proposed Bible story book for young children, and I used my typed pages, which had already come back from the typesetter, to teach Lori. She could keep them and re-read them at home.

We started the first simple story, "God makes Light." Would it be *too* simple for her? She must have learned *something* about God's creating the world somewhere in her life. We read in the story that:

> Long ago, in the beginning, God was there. God always was. He has no beginning and no ending. We call Him *eternal.* That is very hard for us to understand, isn't it? God is holy and pure and perfect, and without any thought of wickedness in Him; and because He is holy and pure and perfect, He knows what is best. We call Him *wise.* And God is so great that He has all the power. He knows what is best and He can do what is best.
> Do you know what God in His greatness did? He made the world. First, the world was not there, and then the world was there! How could that be? The earth where we live and the heavens where God lives came because God spoke. His powerful Word called the heaven and earth to be made.

We stopped right there. Her face had a look of awe. She pantomimed speaking and then spread out her hands in hills and valleys and smooth places. She turned, questioning, to me. Was it almost too wonderful for her to believe? Meekly she wrote on the board, "Lori not know."

"What did you think?" I wrote.

She shrugged. I wondered — and I still wonder — whether she had heard the creation story when she was young and had not understood it. Had she never considered in her more mature years how our world came into being? I would never know the answer. I could not daydream for long. Lori was hurrying me on to the account of the next creation day, and we finished studying God's work of creation on the first three days.

When she came a week later for her next lesson, she was bubbling over with enthusiasm. Often before our lesson, she tried to stretch the chatting time with notes on the board about her friends. Not today! She was all business. She asked me what we were waiting for. So we plunged into the lesson of creation days four, five, and six. We read about the variety of fish and birds God created on day five. Then came the animals, and we read:

> On the sixth day, God spoke His powerful Word to the *earth* and called all the animals that moved out of the earth. He made three kinds of animals: the wild animals that live in the forests and jungles — like lions, bears, elephants, and zebras; the tame animals that live on farms or are pets — like sheep, horses, dogs, and cats; and the small animals that creep along the ground, which we call *bugs* — like ladybugs, beetles, grasshoppers, and caterpillars.

This is where Lori took over. She wrote and she talked and she shouted. "God made horses?" she asked. They were her favorite animal. She loved to ride. It took too long to write what she wanted to say. She was shouting far louder than she realized, in her own broken chant: "Black horses, brown horses, white horses. . . ." She paused and laughed, "Monkeys? Zoo?"

And there stood my husband in the doorway, from his study across the hall. "Is something wrong?" he asked. "I heard such a commotion and so much noise in my study. . . ."

He got no farther. Lori started on him. "Monkeys!" she shouted. "Lions," and putting her voice in a lower register, said, "Worms." Then came flying motions and "Birds!"

His serious face stopped her. She grabbed the lesson and shoved it into his hand and wrote "God made animals," on the chalk-board; and under it, "Now Lori know."

His face said everything my heart was saying: she is twenty years old and has never understood the creation story, and now she does not know how to express her joy. He looked sad and glad, just as I felt, and as Lori had felt scores of times when she made her amazing discoveries about the Scriptures.

My husband's face did not stay sober long. Lori gave him a hug and a kiss. The ice between the two was broken. "Vite" was no longer a tolerated onlooker: he was her friend.

The epilogue to our lesson came the next Sunday morning in church while Pastor Van Baren was reading the law. Often we who are accustomed to the reading of the law each Lord's Day go through this part of the worship service in a routine way. Not *this* Sunday morning! The pastor was reading, and Lori was following the eraser of the pencil: "For in six days the Lord made heaven, and earth, the sea, and all that in them is, and rested the seventh day..." and Lori exploded. With excited whispers (not soft ones) and gestures, she made me know that now she understood it.

* * * * * * * * * * * * * * * * * * *

Our lessons during the summer were a bit more informal. Because we met in our home, and because she was my friend, and a very inquisitive one, Lori felt impelled to examine her surroundings carefully. At first she asked whether she might open drawers or peek in closets, or snitch something from the refrigerator. But soon she had the run of the house, and within reason, because of her diabetes, she helped herself to a goody from the refrigerator. Once when she took a cookie, I wrote on our pad, "You're welcome, Lori Hoeksema." Not at all abashed, she laughed her loud "a-a-h-h," and gestured that I had 1, 2, 3 4 children, and one more finger — Lori — made 5. I had not realized she felt so much at home.

At least once during each lesson, when she was tired of concentrating and needed a break (she seemed more tired in hot weather, and I was delegated to fetch a glass of diet 7-up) or when something in the lesson struck her, she shoved back our "junk," as she called it, and made a gesture of opening a door and giving a kiss, followed by the quick "ring finger — hair — Vite" routine. At first she had wanted to barge into his study at will. I explained that he was a busy man, and if we bother him, we knock first. "Only one time in a lesson," I warned her. She answered: "Lori know — busy — knock — many rules." I had not thought of our home in that way. But she accepted our rules as she accepted everything else in her life.

* * * * * * * * * * * * * * * * * * *

Lori was very conscious of time. She always dated her papers, and whether we were talking about a birthday party or an outing at Ottawa Beach, she meticulously included the time, the day, and the date. Her news items at our talk time often read like this: "Go to grandma — 5 p.m. — Friday — July 15, 1983 — stay overnight."

For a girl with Lori's handicaps, she had remarkable comprehension of time and space; these assets stood her in good stead when we studied Old Testament history that summer. She communicated to me that in her mind she could easily back up from the New Testament lessons about the life of Jesus to the stories at the beginning of time.

We were ready to take up the history of Adam and Eve. How would she react to the entrance of sin into the world? That she knew *sin* by observation and experience she had told me dozens of times. But she probably never had heard how it entered our world. As we read the story of the beautiful paradise where God had put Adam and Eve, and described the garden where all was perfect and nothing died, and saw an Adam and Eve who did nothing wrong, but lived perfectly with God, her body swayed

66

with the rhythm of the words we were reading. Suddenly she had a jolt. She read that the devil, inside a snake, came into paradise and told a wicked lie.

She hesitated, but decided to follow the eraser, and read on. "*God* had told them not to eat of the fruit of the tree of knowledge of good and evil, for if they did, they would die; and the *devil* told them to eat of it, for if they did, they would be like God. The devil told a wicked lie. He said, 'Ye shall not surely die.' Eve should have looked at the tree with obedient eyes, but she began to look at it with sinful eyes. She reached out her hand, took some fruit, and gave Adam some, too. Now they both had sinned."

Lori stopped reading and said, clearly enough for me to understand, "Oh, bad — bad." She repeated it and shoved the lesson sheet away. She had never known how sin entered the world!

"Read on, Lori," I wrote. "Good news coming," but she paid no attention. She tapped me, and with a series of quick motions, she told me what was in her mind. She touched my ring, her hair, and said "Vite," and knocked. So off we went across the hall, Lori with her lesson in her hand.

Quietly and soberly she stood inside the door, holding her lesson. I could tell by the way she looked at us that she knew that we had known this truth all our lives, but she needed sympathy for another of her shocking discoveries.

"What's the matter, Lori?" my husband asked. She held up her lesson, and said again, "Oh, bad — bad!"

They read the paragraph together, and she was ready to leave again. The dear girl just wanted to tell him that she knew now. She had to share it with "Vite."

We were ready to continue the lesson. I had been trying to get her to read our lessons orally, and she began voicing the words that told her that Adam and Eve *knew* they had sinned and were ashamed and tried to hide from God; but that God always finds His children — I made sure Lori knew that Adam and Eve were still God's children. She nodded, but her troubled face still held questions.

So we went on. She read that God always does what He says He will do. He kept His Word of warning that "in the day that thou eatest thereof thou shalt surely die." Now came the task of making clear to her what *death* is: not that they stopped breathing and dropped dead, but that their *hearts* died to God and turned to evil, so that they *hated* the good and *loved* the evil. They lived *away* from God's face, and God says that to live apart from Him is death. Because Adam and Eve sinned, they passed that sin on to everyone who was born since then in the world.

I asked, "Do you understand that kind of death, Lori?"

She understood it only too well. She was pointing to her heart and slowly nodding her head. We read three more sentences: "God made clothes for Adam and Eve from the skins of animals. Do you know why? When God killed the animals He was making a picture of Jesus, Who some day would die for their sins."

She asked on the board, "Take a long time?"

She picked up her Bible and we shuffled through the pages of the long history of God's people before Christ came, and Lori knew the answer.

We had one more paragraph to go: "Remember, because Adam and Eve sinned, we are born sinful, too. The promise of Jesus to die on the cross is for *us,* too. He saves all His children from their sins."

She sighed and pointed to her head. She had anticipated the

ending. I sighed, too. The story of Adam and Eve's fall into sin had never made such a dramatic impact on me as it made this afternoon as I taught my Lori. Her disappointment and sadness at the magnitude of the first sin and its awesome results for the history of the world loomed blacker, as God's grace beamed brighter for me — all because of a girl who had never heard the story before.

Now she knew the story of the beginning and the end of our salvation. We had a lot of ground to cover in between.

* * * * * * * * * * * * * * * * * * * *

When we spent time chatting about family, friends, and especially babies, Lori had her own quick way of identifying them. In her immediate family, she said "faa - er" rather well, in a lower pitched voice. Mother was a very fast "mo-ther," with an index finger on her lower lip — I never learned why. In clipped tones, when she talked about her family, she said, "Deb, *Ran*-dy, *Tra*-cy," but it was easier to use signs for her brother and sisters. And sometimes Lori liked to use the easy way. When she wanted to tell me something about Debbie, the oldest (under Lori), she held her palm outspread just above her head, for Randy her palm was at eye level, and for Tracy about chin level. I knew what she meant, but was concerned that she was not using her voice. Could I prod her to use her voice more? It seemed her voice would atrophy through disuse.

Although I was aware that I was asked to teach her Bible lessons and help with her spiritual growth, I could not teach only a mind. I must teach a whole girl, one of the best on the face of the earth. I could try to help her with one of her other outstanding difficulties: her lack of clear speech. If only we could use the little ability she had and improve her speech! If I decided I could not understand her signs, she would be *forced* to use her voice.

The next time she came and we started with some friendly conversation, she identified someone as above her head and someone else at chin level. I motioned that I did not understand. (I did.) She told me again, and included a third person at eye level this time. Again I pointed to my head and shook it. In exasperation, she said, "Randy." I laughed when I gave my "Oh!" of understanding.

She wrote "trick" on the board and tickled me. Then we had a serious talk together.

"Are you trying hard enough to use your voice, Lori?"

She shook her head.

"Shall we work on it a little harder? If you can say their names, don't use signs."

"Teach girls *Bible*?" She was adept at changing the subject.

Immediately worried that she had offended me, she wrote "OK," but I could see that she wrote it with some reluctance. It seemed almost too much of an effort for her to learn to speak with any semblance of clarity.

We practiced anyway, as we chatted about her family, and especially when we took up our lessons in Old Testament history. I expected her to read the whole lesson orally by this time, with special emphasis on the names we met. "A-bra-ham" was fairly easy, but "Ja-cob" was always a tough one, because of the *J* followed by the long *a*, an impossible combination for her. Through all the lessons we studied together from then on, she read orally; but her vocal chords were badly impaired, and we did not see much improvement in her speech.

Lori always hoped that her mother (who transported her this summer of '83) would be late to pick her up. After our lesson we wandered through the yard, finding and eating raspberries, and picking roses for her to take home. Lori had a sense of the artistic. She always tried to match the colors of the roses she cut

70

to the outfit she was wearing. After the ceremony of rose-cutting, she carefully selected some perfect asparagus ferns for greenery and started working on the arrangement. She worked with the rhythm of her whole body, with the involuntary gasps and sighs of a deaf girl, and always achieved an artisitc arrangement. The roses were the highlight of our free time. If we chatted too long in my office after the lesson, she brought me up short by writing, "You forgetful or something?" And we would scramble for tools and run for the rose garden.

* * * * * * * * * * * * * * * * * * *

Each Sunday during that summer, we met Lori for the morning and evening services. Although we knew and felt the work of the Holy Spirit in our lessons together, Lori's words and actions in church services confirmed it in striking ways. I had ceased to worry about writing prayers with abstract concepts, because Lori understood sin and grace, blessing and faith. . . and was fast learning many more spiritual concepts. She also knew how to address the Father she could not see, just as she grasped *ideas* which she could not see.

Lori's comments written at the end of her prayers convinced me of a fact I already knew: that the Spirit filled the lack in the prayers I had written, and taught her. During the summer, she was always eager to get "her prayer," as we in the congregation bowed our heads. After repeated warnings to read the prayer quietly and not interrupt me during prayer, I gave in and let her nudge me occasionally.

This is how it would go: I wrote instructions at the beginning, and followed them with the prayer. At the end, I made suggestions such as "read the prayer again," or "write your own prayer now," or "pray your own prayer." Then Lori would settle down. On this particular Sunday she read in her instructions, "Remember, when we pray, we say 'Thee' and 'Thou' to God because He is so holy." Shortly after that she tentatively poked me, took up her pencil when I responded, and read the first part of the prayer with me: "Dear Lord, it is time to pray to Thee again. It is always a happy time when we can come and talk with Thee. Thou art our Friend and our Father, and we may tell Thee anything we want to. We always want to thank Thee because *Thou art so very good to us* (she had underlined it). Thou hast given us our health and our food and our families and this wonderful world to live in. We know, too, that *Thou dost always care for us* (underlined by Lori again) because Thou dost never sleep."

She wanted to share God's care with me, and when I had finished following her eraser to the end of the paragraph, she hugged her prayer and went on. How could I have stern rules for a girl like this?

All was quiet, relatively, for a while, and then came a loudly whispered "Oh," and another nudge. I frowned, but she persisted. We read, "When I have troubles, teach me to tell Thee about them and teach me to trust in Thee to help me with my troubles." These words were underlined, too. The next sentence was, "Teach me to pray for all Thy people and to love them." What Lori wanted to know was, "Pray now?" and she made motions of folding her hands. I nodded, and could hear her lips making their laborious sounds as she was learning to pray her own prayer for those she loved.

Having Lori sit with me distracted in a measure from my concentration and enjoyment of the service, but the rewards were well worth it. I hoped, however, that she would settle down now. It wasn't to be. She held up the last paragraph of the prayer: "Bless us all in church this morning. Be with the minister who must preach Thy Word, and make Thy people here happy to worship Thee with all those who love Thy holy name." She kept her finger on one word: *happy*.

Three interruptions in one prayer, and Lori and I were both happy!

Lori especially loved prayers on themes — she enjoyed the symbolism: Jesus as the Bread of Life, or as the Lamb of God. She enjoyed themes such as our lives being one long path, with Jesus as our Guide, and one of her favorites was the figure of God's people being living stones, which He uses to build His house. The idea that God used *stones* to teach us spiritual truths intrigued her, and she came back to that figure often. It showed the depths of thought she was able to reach.

Lori's prayers often addressed her deafness, and helped her understand why it was good that the Lord had made her deaf. In another prayer she read, "The Bible says that our Lord, Who is our Shepherd, leads us in the path of righteousness. It is the path of our life. I know that Thou art my Shepherd Who has led me in the path of being deaf. Thou hast led me on a special path in my life, O Lord. I do not know why, but Thou dost know why: because it is a good path for me. . . ."

She wanted to share these few lines with me, and as I read, she meditatively stroked my arm. What was she thinking? I looked at her bowed head, with its neatly styled hair, and my Lori was nodding her head in agreement.

Sometimes she was not in the mood for concentration and hard work in church, for it *was* hard work for her to participate. Sometimes she felt like looking around at her friends, re-reading the bulletin, and giving her prayer the once-over-lightly. When she read the following words at the end of another prayer, she let me know that she felt chastened, although I had not intended them in a negative sense. She read: "Now bless the minister as he preaches to Thy people. And when I copy words from the Bible, give me the Holy Spirit in my heart so that I can understand and love those words."

She wrote, "Do better — try hard in church." She did.

People asked me often, "How old do you think Lori is mentally?"

St matthew 6

24 No man can serve two master for either
He will hate the one and love the other or else
He will hold to the one and despise the
~~other Ye cannot serve God and mammon~~

Anxiety and God's Kingdom
25 Therefore I say unto you Take no thought
for your life what ye shall eat or what ye shall
drink nor yet for your body what ye shall put
on Is not the life more than meat and the body
than raiment 26 Behold the fowls of the air
for they snow not neither do they reap nor
gather into barns yet your heavenly father
feedeth them are ye not much better than
they (27 which of you by taking thought can
add one cubit unto his stature?
28 And why take ye thought for raiment Conside
the lilies of the field how they grow they to
not neither do they spin
29 and yet I say unto you That even solo mor
in all his glory was not arrayed like one of
these 30 wherefore if God so clothe the
grass of the field which today is and
tomorrow is cast into the oven shall
He not much more clothe you O ye of
little faith

I was not at all sure. When she teased and clowned and when we were silly together she was about eight. When she mingled with the young people and joined in their conversations, she was about eighteen. When she studied her lessons with me and jolted me with her increasingly deep insights, she was at least twenty-eight. So I answered my friends, "I'm not sure if it's eight or eighteen or twenty-eight."

Chapter 7

Lori In a New Church Home

When our summer lessons were over and we had gone as far as we could in Old Testament history in one summer, Lori went to the bin in my office where we stored the four by six cards with our prayers printed on them. She pointed to herself, and then made two swings of her arm in the direction of Byron Center. Two swings of her arm indicated the distance to her home. I nodded. She was welcome to take the cards home now.

"Big pack," she said, quite clearly; and eyes shining, she hugged and kissed the pack, made her gesture for bed-time, and repeated in abbreviated form: "Mon., Tue., Wed., Thur., Fri., Sat., Sun." She had a good supply of new prayers again. Her reactions of genuine delight to the small pleasures in her life, especially as they concerned her growth in grace, still caught me off-guard. What other young girl would react this way to a few cards with prayers? But for Lori, there seemed to be an inner urgency to have them and to use them, to make up for lost time.

Then she thought of something, put the cards down, and made motions of typing. "You?" she asked. It was not the first time she had shown appreciation for the work I did for her. Every now and then, as she surveyed a lesson, she would pantomime typing and express with her face and motions of her hands that she knew how *much* work it must have been, and then sink down in mock exhaustion into her chair. This time, without waiting for an answer, she bordered the chalkboard with the word *Love* and in the middle printed, "Mrs. Hoekeman." She was so thankful, I hadn't the heart to tell her she misspelled my name again. Poor girl: she had never heard that long Dutch name pronounced.

* * * * * * * * * * * * * * * * * *

After a break of a few weeks from our lessons, it was October again, and we were back in Room 3 in Hudsonville Church with the other girls on Monday evenings.

Autumn brought the things that Lori enjoyed so much in life. Best were birthdays and holidays. In our chats about Thanksgiving and Christmas, I had to hear not only about the ceremonies of gift giving, but mostly about the meals: the appetizers, the huge bowls of mashed potatoes, the turkey, and the total enjoyment of being with a large group of relatives.

Birthdays were almost as important. Already in the summer time, she speculated where father would take the family for dinner on October 14 to celebrate. She kept reminding me of her birthday and I kept telling her that mine came first, on October 6. When that date finally arrived, she gave me a card and a lovely gift, but immediately asked on the board, "You send me a card?"

Although I liked to tease her, I couldn't tease her about *this* birthday, such a special one, her twenty-first! I promised.

Then she wrote: "Lori many friends — love cards — like 100 cards on 21 birthday — important."

"That would be great, Lori," I wrote, and set about to make her wish come true. After class, I asked Pastor Van Baren, still Lori's "good man," to stay a moment. When I told him about my Lori's wish, I did not have to suggest what to do.

"I'll make a little announcement about it on Sunday's bulletin. It will give people plenty of time to get cards to her by Friday, the fourteenth." This is the notice that appeared on the bulletin of Sunday, October 9, 1983: *"Happy Birthday!* One of the 'special' children of the congregation, Lori Holstege, celebrates her 21st birthday on Friday, Oct. 14. She has spoken wistfully of receiving as many as 100 birthday cards on this special occasion. Perhaps she can receive many, many more with your help!" and then followed her address.

Lori almost reached her goal. More than eighty cards from her relatives and friends were delivered to her home.

* * * * * * * * * * * * * * * * * * * *

On October 20, 1983, a new congregation in Byron Center was organized. The Hudsonville congregation was getting almost too big for its auditorium, and Byron Center became a daughter congregation. Because Lori's family lived in Byron Center, they would naturally transfer their membership to the new Byron Center congregation. The time was ripe for a new congregation there, but when the Holsteges transferred, Lori and I would have different church homes. I was not very happy about that. The problem lay in the worship services. During the past year she had become dependent on my help for full participation in worship services, and she had enjoyed the experience so tremendously. If she stopped learning in church now, she would stop growing.

At our next lesson, after the organization was a fact, Lori was enthusiastic about the new congregation. She wrote, "Good — new church — Byron Center — meet at Byron Center Christian Junior High."

Had she thought of the problem? I brought it up, explaining that we can not sit together in church anymore, because I will go to Hudsonville and she will go to Byron Center, and that I *must* go to Hudsonville because I belong with my husband and to Hudsonville's congregation. She will go to Byron. We cannot sit together anymore.

Lori passed over the problem rather lightly. All she wrote was, "Sit Lori sometimes — Byron." Our forced separation had not yet made an impact on her.

I was very concerned. If she did not get consistent training, she would not advance in learning nor in grace, she would not be satisfied, and she would lose her joy of worshipping with her fellow believers. We agreed, for the time being, that when my husband filled the pulpit for vacancies in other congregations, and I could not sit in the pew with him anyway, I would come to Byron Center and sit with Lori. For the first few weeks he was busy with preaching assignments. I attended the new Byron Center congregation with Lori.

Then came the Sunday when my husband and I were to attend Hudsonville again. That week I had given Lori some materials to keep her busy doing the "Lord's work" during her service in Byron Center; and I was ready to leave for church that Sunday morning. It was almost nine o'clock. The telephone rang. I answered and was puzzled. I couldn't understand a thing. Then my heart sank. It was Lori! She said something that started with a *b* sound. Was something wrong?

I hung up and dialed their number. Her father answered.

"Is something wrong with Lori?" I asked.

"Oh, did she call you?" he asked calmly. "No, nothing is wrong. She just wanted you to sit with her in Byron Center this morning. She knows you can't, but you know Lori — she is quite insistent."

"Jay, I belong in my own church."

"You're right. Lori has to learn to understand. Go to Hudsonville and think no more of it."

But I did. My husband was very quiet on our way to Hudsonville. So was I.

"Poor Lori," he finally said. "I wonder whether you made the right decision."

I cried. I *thought* I had made the right decision. But I did not enjoy the service that morning. I kept thinking of Lori. Over a dinner that I can't remember tasting, we discussed where my duty lay, but we could not resolve the dilemma.

80

That week we were scheduled for our annual visit from our pastor and an elder of our Hudsonville congregation. The elder who came was the father of one of the girls I was teaching and very sympathetic to the problems of the care and education of handicapped children. During the visit, when they asked if I had any questions or problems, I brought up my problem of church attendance, and after talking about the situation for a while, we reached a conclusion of sorts. For the time being, the pastor and the elder thought, it would be best for me to attend the Byron Center worship services with Lori as often as possible—whenever my husband was preaching elsewhere, and otherwise probably one service a Sunday. The elder, knowing first-hand about difficulties such as these, said I would never be criticized for missing the services at Hudsonville.

When I explained it to Lori, and she knew our services together would not be as regular as in the days when we both attended Hudsonville, she put her arm over my shoulder, and her face plainly showed "what must be must be."

In practice, it did not work well. At one of our lessons, we probed the possibility of teaching Lori's father all our now-perfected details for effective participation in the church services, and having him take over; but Lori, absolute as usual, turned thumbs down. She made herself slow and limp. She was probably correct. Her father was not quick and dynamic enough.

"Eunice?" Lori suggested. Eunice and her husband (and Lori's favorites, Jonathan and David) also attended the new Byron Center congregation; but Eunice had two young sons to care for during services, besides being a pianist. No, Eunice could not do it.

"Marcia?" she ventured next. "Like Tom." Lori liked the kind, sympathetic ways of Marcia's youngest son, and she never forgot that they had a "Mayo Clinic experience" in common. Aunt Marcia, vivacious and dedicated, with her husband and family had also transferred from Hudsonville to Byron Center. Aunt Marcia was the solution, and she was Lori's church partner from then on.

Very soon the Byron Center congregation had a new minister. Young Pastor Barry Gritters accepted their call. Pastor Gritters soon began to take an intense interest in Lori, and started making outlines of his sermons for her, with blanks for her to fill in, along with prayers, as guides for Marcia and Lori. I turned over the cards for the liturgical parts of the service to Marcia and taught her our procedure. Our problem of Lori's participation in the worship services was solved. And Lori was satisfied and happy, she told me.

I was glad that part of my work load, the supervising of Lori's worship services, had been lifted, for I was working on other plans for Lori. Earlier during the fall, when she was still anticipating her twenty-first birthday on October 14, she had written notes to me with increasing frequency. "Lori 21 — special — be grown-up member — God's church." Although we did not mention it at that time, we both had unspoken recollections of that dark night in the narthex of Hudsonville Church. It was time for me to make some long-range plans to make Lori's dream come true.

For the fall and winter of 1983, even though Lori was now a member of the Byron Center congregation, for convenience' sake we still met in Room 3 of Hudsonville Church, and Lori was glad to see her old friends and visit with them as usual before and after class. We continued our study of Old Testament history. She loved to read the stories of Israel in Egypt, but detested Pharaoh as much as she had detested the Pharisees of Jesus' day. She showed malicious glee when the Lord sent the plagues, each one worse than the one before. As she did in her other lessons, she reacted with the most interest to the deeper, spiritual meaning of the historical events of Scripture. And although I should have known it by this time, she always caught me by surprise with her eagerness to delve below the surface of the historical events and find God's purpose in them. In her lesson I wrote that the people of Israel were God's children who were slaves in Egypt, the *house of sin*. They could not get out by themselves, just as we are God's children in a *world of sin* and we cannot leave our world of sin, either, by ourselves. Her eyes lit up with understanding, and she waited for the conclusion.

She read, "Now the Israelites were leaving Egypt, which was a picture of the house of sin, and they were going back to Canaan, which was a picture of the house of His love.

"We are on our way to Canaan, too. Another name for Canaan is heaven. In heaven we will live with God in love forever."

Lori understood not only that the Old Testament Canaan was a type of heaven for the Israelites. She knew that the land of Canaan is just as real a picture for *us*. She wrote, "Jesus too — angels," and gave me her sign of understanding as she added these details to the picture of her future home.

I discovered another aptitude in this girl of many surprises. She had an excellent grasp of map work. "Good in geog. at school," she had written, and began begging for map worksheets. If I had allowed it, she would have pored over the Bible atlas for half the lesson. Her maps, as we started charting the Israelites' wilderness wanderings, were works of art.

When we came to Mount Sinai, it was difficult for me to make lessons which taught her to understand God's law. True, she read the law from her card each Sunday morning, but we had never delved into meanings, and it was time for her to know the practical application of the law to her life as Lori, living in the Holstege family.

I did not know that Lori had the same concern I had, but she let me know. As soon as she looked at her worksheet, she clapped the flat of her hand on the table, too loudly, and sat back and sighed, as if to say, "At last!" She pointed to her head and shook it and caricatured her "stupid" face, adding a series of meaningless dronings, which I took to be her interpretation of the measure of her understanding of the law. She *hadn't* understood, and was eager to delve into its meaning.

After we had studied the commandments somewhat in depth, she reacted as my other handicapped girls did. She approached God's law with utter candidness, and told me which command she had the most trouble obeying: "Honor thy father and thy mother. . . ." With a troubled face, she reached for the chalk and wrote, "Bad — mad — stubborn — stamp." It was hard for her, even though it troubled her, to give up her strong-willed ways. Lori and I spent most of our time during that class with her problems of being headstrong and of going her own way, and at the same time being the Lori who wanted to love and obey her parents for God's sake. She read in the lesson:

> The fifth commandment says, "Honor thy father and thy mother." *Honor* means to do what they tell you to do. Another word is *obey.* Sometimes you and I don't *want* to obey them. Right? Sometimes we get mad. God says that is wrong. Why must you do what your father and mother tell you to do? Because *God* wants you to. And nothing else is important. Only God is. When you do what father and mother tell you to do, you are doing what *God* wants you to do. It is sin if you do not obey, and God *hates* sin.

The Lord helped her to obey this commandment, and it showed on the outside, because members of her family told me, "We notice a difference in Lori. She *tries* to obey."

She grasped one more concept: the two tables of the law. The first, how we must love and obey God; and the second, how we must act toward our neighbors. Our lesson ended with the following: "Lori, when our Lord Jesus was on the earth, someone asked Him, 'Master, which is the great commandment of the law?'

84

"And Jesus answered him, 'Thou shalt love the Lord thy God with all thy heart, and with all thy soul, and with all thy mind. This is the first and great commandment. And the second is like unto it. Thou shalt love thy neighbor as thyself.'

"You will find Jesus' words in the book of Matthew, chapter 22, verses 36, 37, 38. Read them in your Bible.

"Read this lesson with father. Think hard about it, for it is very important for a Christian young girl. It is how you must live!"

Later I found the passage from Matthew copied on her papers very often. That passage was to crop up again in a future lesson.

Chapter 8

Lori Gets Ready

Through the winter months, Lori studied the history of the Israelites' wanderings in the desert and their conquest of Canaan under Joshua. In the spring of 1984, Lori's father and I had a conference. We reviewed her progress and understanding of Old Testament history. Lori had had lessons for only a little longer than a year, and I would not have believed a year earlier that I would be saying to her father, "In some ways, Lori is very profound." He agreed.

Then I laid out my plans. I believed that Lori was ready for doctrinal studies and said to him, "With your permission, I would like to start her on the Heidelberg Catechism."

I thought he would be surprised, but he wasn't. He had rather expected it, and he later told me he had anticipated my next suggestion: "I would like to prepare her for public confession of faith."

Barely containing our emotions, we faced this big step in her life which Lori was about to take. We knew it would be necessary for me to confer with Pastor Gritters as to the method, and then submit my proposal to Lori's consistory for their approval. We faced some obstacles: how do the elders examine a deaf-mute with questions of doctrine and faith? How will a retarded (but not nearly as retarded as most people think) and frightened girl react in a gathering of the rulers of her congregation? The best way might be to ask them to accept Lori's tests and my progress reports as the basis for their decision on Lori's doctrinal competence. It was wise, we thought, to leave this far-reaching decision to the future, when we would have a better perspective of Lori's progress, and then get Pastor Gritters' advice.

Pastor Gritters and I met to discuss the details. We notified the Byron Center council and obtained their blessing to start lessons on the Heidelberg Catechism with Lori. On Monday, April 30, we did not have our usual lesson on Old Testament history, but an explanation of the scope of the doctrines she would soon be learning, and the importance for the rest of her life of the big step she was about to take. This is what Lori and I read and discussed together:

No test today, Lori. Instead, I want to tell you about something very important. Will you read *slowly* and *carefully*?

Lori, you are a different kind of girl from the one you were before you learned all about God and His Words in the Bible, before I taught you. I taught you almost two years now, and I can see the difference in you. Can you tell, inside yourself, that you are different now? That you love the Lord more? That you understand His Word better? That God's Spirit in your heart teaches you how to be a Christian young girl? (With each sentence she read, Lori pantomimed her response, showing her understanding and her love for her Lord, in a way that only Lori could express it.)

Lori, you have grown up a lot in the last two years, and now it is *almost time* for you to act like a grown-up *member* of God's church. A *member* is a *person — you*.

Do you know how to be a grown-up member of God's church at Byron Center? By *confessing your faith*. Let me tell you about it. *Faith* is what you *believe*. *Confessing your faith* is telling the whole church about it.

How do you do that?

1. You have to learn more about God and the Bible. I will teach you and you will try hard.

2. Do you know what you have to learn? More of the things that God told His church to believe. We call it *the truth*. Another word is *doctrine*. Say it.

3. You already have learned some doctrines, so it will not be so hard for you. One is the truth — the doctrine — about God. We will study that lesson again so you can remember. (Earlier we had had a lesson on "Who God is," to help Lori understand His works and His Word.)

4. Another is about how sinful we are, and yet how God says we have to obey His perfect law. You know about that, too, don't you?

5. Another doctrine is that God chose *some people*, His *church*, to be His own people, and that He did not choose most of the people on the earth. They are the wicked sinners who do not believe God's Word.

88

6. Another doctrine is that God sent Jesus to this earth to die for His own people, and *only* for His own people, by spilling His blood on the cross and dying for them, so they do not have to die in hell. We call that our *salvation.* Salvation means *being saved.*

7. Another doctrine is that God has prepared heaven for all His own people, and He takes us there after we die, to live forever in happiness with Him; but He puts all the wicked people into hell, where they will suffer forever for their sins.

8. You must still learn the doctrine of *baptism.* You must learn *why* you were baptized when you were a baby, and why all babies in God's church are baptized. I know you will love to learn about this. (Lori gasped, "Oh!" and picked up her pencil and wrote under the words of Number 8: "Deb Lubbers — girl baby — Carmen Dawn — Butterwroth — Friday home," complete with misspelling).

9. One more doctrine you must still learn about is the doctrine of the Lord's Supper — about the bread and the wine.

Then, after you understand it and make confession of your faith, the elders of the church will let you take the bread and wine, too.

We will have to study these *doctrines,* but it will be a happy time, because these doctrines are easy to learn and they are so beautiful.

Would you like to try to learn enough to be a grown-up child of God, and to confess your faith in front of the people of Byron Center Church? _____ (Lori solemnly wrote "yes" on the blank, and then looked frightened. She quickly pointed to herself and to me, held hands for togetherness, and I nodded that I would help her, of course. To seal our pact, she printed "Mrs. Hoekeman and Lori" underneath the sentence. We went on reading.) It is a very important and serious thing to do. You must do your best to learn and I will help you get ready to confess your faith.

It will take a lot of weeks, but we can work it out together. All right? _____ She wrote another "yes."

You should talk this over with father, too. I think he will be happy that his Lori wants to be a *full* member of God's church, don't you?

Do you think you can pray to God in your mind and your heart about it and ask Him to help you learn? _____ (Lori wrote "yes.")

The atmosphere was much more solemn and intense than usual, and as we came near to the end, her tears slowly dripped onto the paper. She reached for a tissue and kept going. The tears kept coming and I thought she was probably overwhelmed by the preparations and at the same time was shedding tears of sheer joy. I was right. She wrote: "Much work." Then she ran her hand up the paper to Number 7. Under the word "happiness" in that paragraph, she had written "Happy." Now she pointed to it.

We started our lessons in doctrine in early summer. Lori was not yet finished with Old Testament history, and we decided that she would take one Bible story each week, and study it by herself. The following week I would quiz her on it. That would leave most of our lesson time for studying the Heidelberg Catechism. The plan worked well.

* * * * * * * * * * * * * * * * * * * *

Friday, the 27th of April, was a happy day for all of us. On that day the long-awaited Bible story book, *Come, Ye Children,* came out. Because Lori had often tried to make our house her second home, she had watched each step in the progress and production of the book: she examined the proofs, and passed judgment on the artwork. On the evening of April 27, a beautifully groomed Lori walked into Hudsonville Church. The public was invited to a "get acquainted" evening. Jeff, the artist, had mounted the two hundred original illustrations, and the people who came had the opportunity to purchase an illustration of their choice; and Jeff and I were available for autographing. Proud Lori walked around with the two illustrations she had chosen and which her father and grandfather had bought for her, and with her autographed book, with special words of love written in it.

For her first picture Lori chose the small, simple illustration from the story, "Two Spies Go To Jericho," which shows the two spies as two tiny specks against the forbidding landscape and the high, thick walls of Jericho.

"Why would Lori choose a picture like this?" her father asked me, as he held it up. It was not the dynamic, action-filled

illustration we would expect her to choose. I could not understand, either, but when Lori made up her mind, none of our
questionings prevailed. She wanted *that* picture. Because of
the story?

Of course! It was a story that Lori had *lived* in our lessons not
long ago. The two spies, unprotected, went into this huge
walled city filled with their enemies; and Rahab took them in
and hid them under flax on her roof — a dangerous deed! Then
she told a lie to save them. Lori *liked* Rahab. But after thinking
about my question in her lesson a few weeks earlier, whether it
was *right* for Rahab to tell a lie to save the spies, she had admitted that to tell a lie was wrong. Nonetheless, she admitted
that she, too, would have told a lie to save Joshua's two spies,
even though her face said she would be uneasy about the lie.
She had called them "God's men" on the chalkboard. What
else could Rahab have done than try to save God's men? She
pantomimed their escape through the window on the wall,
their race back to Joshua, and their breathless arrival.

Now she had chosen the illustration of the unprotected men of
God in their dangerous, hostile surroundings. Is that the way
Lori felt sometimes — in hostile surroundings? And the reason
she chose that picture? Perhaps, but I don't know.

The other illustration she chose was from the story "Israel
Wins the Victory at Ai." The illustration shows Joshua's warriors
in the foreground, ready to attack the burning city, which had
been set on fire by the ambush in the rear. Lori mimicked the
postures of Joshua's soldiers in the illustration, but the best
part of the picture was Joshua stretching out his spear towards
the city of Ai through the whole battle, a picture of the Lord's
hand stretched out to help His people. During our lesson she
had cheered for the victories of God's people! Lori *loved* to
learn about God's care and help for His people.

We forfeited our regular lesson material at our next session, and spent our time getting acquainted with the new book. From now on she could study Old Testament history, not from a manuscript, but from the finished product. With the penchant for details of a young child, she delighted in the artist's fine touches in the illustrations and recognized his subtle humor. We read one of the stories together, just to get the feel of the book, and then our time was up. Before she left, Lori picked up the chalk and once again bordered the chalkboard with *Love* around the four edges. In the center she wrote:

"Thank God for
Mrs. Hoekeman
Writes book for girls."

A simple thank you with simple piety, and with my name misspelled as usual — that was my Lori!

When I decided on the long-range project of making a Bible story quilt, Jeff gave me permission to use his original illustrations. I photo-copied them and traced them on quilt squares. Lori knew all about it and was eager to help engineer the project. We had finished our classes in Room 3 for the season, and were meeting in my office again. Often I had the quilt squares laid out on the living room floor, and Lori came early and stayed late to give advice or be my cheering section for the project. Her eye for detail was better than mine, and she knew it. She teased me and tickled me, and chucked me under the chin as we carefully crawled over the pinned squares, until my husband came in to investigate the commotion. Seeing his face, she got up from the floor, tickled him in passing, and went for the note pad in the kitchen. She wrote: "Name — Lori Hoekeman," and handed it to me.

I wrote back, "Can't be. You can't even spell your last name right."

Without missing a beat or acknowledging my criticism, she quickly changed the subject: "Roses?" she wrote.

92

* * * * * * * * * * * * * * * * * * * *

In our craft party that May we had made decorative plates for our mothers. Each of the girls was given a circle of special paper and each drew a design or picture on it with a choice of various media. They understood that after their drawings were finished, I would send their circles away and they would be transferred to plates for their mothers. After I gave the instructions, we spent some time planning our pictures.

Lori was quiet and did not participate very much. I motioned: "Do you know what you're going to do?"

She gave a perfunctory nod. I wasn't needed. The design was already finished in her mind.

"Know your colors?" I asked. She nodded.

We went to work. All we heard from Lori were her usual gasps of effort and concentration.

Suddenly Betty shrieked, "Oh, Lori's is beautiful!"

It was. Lori had taken a stencil of a fat little bird, measured

how often she could place it around the edges of her circle, and began her tracing. Soon six birds were circling her plate. She knew her colors! They were blue birds, with a few brown accents — delicate and pleasing to the eye. The center of her plate was still blank.

"Bub?" she asked. I didn't understand. She made motions of carrying something. A baby? "No," her face said as she shook her head disdainfully. I still didn't understand. Neither did the girls. Whenever Lori went to church or church functions, even to craft parties, she always took her Bible and lesson folder along. She was coming to church, after all! Now she was searching for it in all the clutter, and the moment it dawned on me *what* she was looking for, Lori had found what she was looking for: her *Bible*. What would she want that for?

"Text," she commanded.

I pointed to the blue birds, then to the Bible, flopped my arms in flying motions, and put a questioning expression on my face. Yes, she wanted a text about a bird. What text would Lori want?

After rejecting my first choices, she suddenly said "Aha!" as I showed her Psalm 84:3, and she copied on her circle: "Even the sparrow hath found a house, and the swallow a nest," in perfect lettering in brown.

Betty was right: "Lori's is always the best!"

* * * * * * * * * * * * * * * * * * * *

These happy times were pleasant interludes in our rather strict regimen of lessons and studies of ever-increasing difficulty. Of course, when Lori came in the summertime, there was always so much to tell me in our free time before our lessons: the end-of-the-school-year activities, swimming outings, staying overnight at Grandma Hoezee's house — summer was a great time for Lori!

94

Our lesson time, however, was filled with serious hard work. Through the whole summer and into the fall, we had lessons on the Heidelberg Catechism. We were using a simplified catechism book, *Heidelberg Catechism for Juniors,* with short, concise questions and answers, and easier language for Lori to understand than the long, sometimes involved sentences of the Heidelberg Catechism itself.

I had already explained to her the challenge and importance of these lessons. Her lesson read, in part:

> These lessons are short, but important. We will read them *very slowly* two times because you must know them very well in your mind. Then you must read them two times at home with father or mother. Will you do that? _____ (Lori answered: Yes, 1 week.)
>
> Always remember that this is some of the most important work you will be doing in your whole life. Will you be very serious about it? (And again Lori agreed.)

During the summer of 1984 I saw an intense Lori. She was required to read her lesson aloud, and she usually rocked back and forth, using her whole body for the difficult task of understanding the big words. She had a determination I had not seen before.

Our lessons started with the abbreviated questions and answers on the first Lord's Day of the Heidelberg Catechism:

> What is your only comfort in life and death?
> That we belong to our faithful Savior Jesus Christ.

Next to each page of her catechism book I put a key, explaining the hard words and the deeper concepts; and if an answer was too hard to understand, I paraphrased it.

Question six in Lesson One read:

> Have you any other *evidence* that you belong to Him?
> Yes, for He also made me *sincerely willing* to live unto Him.

My key of explanation, to help Lori, read: *"Evidence* means *how do you know* that you belong to Jesus?" and I taught Lori to read it the simplified way: *"How do you know* that you belong to Him?" She *liked* the simplified way! "The answer means that you *try* every day to live like one of Jesus' children (and Lori added: 'be good')."

I knew she would not comprehend the last question and answer of Lesson One:

> How many things are *necessary* for us to know that we may enjoy this comfort?
> Three things: those pertaining to our sins and misery, to the way of our deliverance, and to the expression of our gratitude.

Lori's paraphrase read:

> The question means: *what do you need to know* to be happy in Jesus?
> The three things are:
> 1. our sins: you and I must know how bad our sins are.
> 2. our deliverance is the way that Jesus saved us from our sins — on the cross.
> 3. our gratitude is our thanks to our God for saving us. When we *express* our gratitude, we say "thank you" to God.

We had finished her first lesson on the Heidelberg Catechism! This first lesson — the one I had worried about — had not given her very much trouble. When, with concern on my face, I motioned, "Could you understand it?" she barely looked at me, nodded her head, and looked at her lesson again. I persisted, however: "Did I ask you a stupid question?" I wrote on the board. She merely nodded again, with a poker face. Was she telling me it was easier than she expected, and was she at the same time masking her inner fears?

Lori fell into the routine of reading the question, and as soon as she came to an underlined word, she looked at the key, where I had written the explanation. We encountered the following words in her next lesson, which was more difficult for her:

96

Posterity means all the people who were born from Adam.

She was to read it twice, and go on. When *forbade* met us, she read that it means "that God would *not let* them:" and we read it in the context: "God would *not let* them eat of the tree of knowledge of good and evil." It was hard going, and it would get harder. Even though I made the lessons short, they were intense. She took her review tests with joy and passed them with A's.

* * * * * * * * * * * * * * * * * * * *

In June the entreating little messages started: "Grandville Fabric — maybe go — Eunice?" followed by a detailed description of the dress she would like *this* summer. She emphasized it must be a "dress — church."

We went. Jonathan and David came along again. For the boys, who were a year older now, the newness of shopping for fabric was gone, but not their delight in Lori. With nearly all the searching and commotion of the year before, we had a delightful time selecting a sundress pattern and a print for the dress, with a soft green eyelet for the jacket. Lori insisted that Jonathan and David give their approval to all the details again. The clerks' comments were much the same as those of the previous year: "What a dear girl, and how you love her! And you're not related?"

Jonathan, with a bit of the philosopher in him, answered for all of us, "No. We just act like we are. But we're brothers and sisters of her in our church."

Having a dress made meant several visits to Eunice's home for fittings. Lori was disproportionately large over her hips, and all patterns had to be adjusted. She made the most of her "trying on" sessions, finding goodies, checking on Eunice's recipes, and joining the boys in their projects. Everyone had fun. Lori was such a joy to have around.

On the Fourth of July, Lori's father called that she was in the hospital because of her diabetes problems. Her stomach had been upset the day before when we had our lesson, and she had worsened during the night. Her father said it was not serious, and she would be hospitalized for a few days so the doctors could regulate her dosages of insulin and stabilize her.

I wanted to see her, but was not able to go the next day. So I promised myself I would go the afternoon of the sixth. In the evening newspaper of the fifth of July was a brief notice of a house fire which destroyed all the contents, but no injuries or deaths were reported. The walls were standing, but the inside was a total loss. I looked at the address. It was Lori's address! And she was in the hospital. Did she know?

I tried desperately to contact someone in the family, but the effort ended in failure. I would have to wait until I saw Lori. Early the next afternoon, roses in hand, I went to the hospital. Lori was sitting on the bed, tubed and wired, but looking well. Today the roses came before the kisses. After she was satisfied with our floral arrangement, we hugged one another gingerly, carefully avoiding all her apparatus. Lori told me, with signs, what they had done to her. A nurse came in and helped explain. There was no mention of a fire. Yet.

The nurse left and Lori hopped out of bed and picked up a news- paper clipping from her table. So she knew! We read it together, sitting on the bed, dangling our legs.

"Are you upset?" I asked on the pad I had taken along.

She wrote, "All gone — inside burn up."

She did not seem very perturbed. Did she realize what this fire had done to her home? She wrote again, "God take care."

Lori said it before I had a chance to take out my card with a message of encouragement for my Lori who had so many hard- ships in her life. We read the message and agreed that God would take care of her and her family. But how would she feel when she saw the burned-out shell of her house?

That evening I talked with her father and he explained that they had come home from the fireworks on the Fourth of July, stuck the key in the latch, opened the door, and flames exploded all over. They were not yet sure of the cause. But they had decided to keep the shell of their house, and completely redo the interior. They would live in a large trailer on their property meanwhile.

Lori was well enough for her lesson the next week. "Burn bad," she wrote, and pinched her nose: "Stink!" Then, "trailer good." She let me know that most of her clothes, her new dress included, plus her lessons, were at her mother's apartment; and she dismissed the subject and suggested we start the lesson. Although she must have been shocked when she saw the actual damage, she seemed rather nonchalant about the fire.

It was a good thing she did not let it bother her. She had a heavy summer ahead of her; we had plans for Lori to confess her faith that fall, if possible.

Pastor Gritters made his promised visit to our class in July. He was vitally interested in Lori and her spiritual progress. For some months he had been writing sermon guides and prayers for her worship services; but he thought he should know more about the approach I used, the vocabulary suitable for Lori, and he wanted to experience Lori's responses first-hand, for he was thinking of easing my teaching load by helping with Lori's instruction in the future. Now he had second thoughts about visiting us. Would his presence distract Lori? No, not Lori. She would show off and do her best at the same time. She was delighted to have a guest whom she was getting to know better each week, and she played to the galleries and outdid herself as Pastor Gritters participated in the lesson. The lovely part of it, Pastor Gritters decided, was that she was so earnest and serious in her showing off. "A most interesting girl," was his remark as he left.

Our lessons continued without let-up that summer. It was August already! Lori kept reminding me that it would be nice if I offered to take her home after lessons sometime. That way there would be no deadlines. The raspberries were ripe again, and there was enough corn for her to take home for the Holsteges' dinner. But those pleasures came only after our sessions of hard work.

We were busy with the second part of the Heidelberg Catechism by this time: our deliverance. Lori understood Who our Mediator is: That He is someone Who is both God and man and Who will die instead of us. She was learning more about the Jesus Who saved her.

It was during the lesson of August 8 (she dated it *Aust 8*) that the fact of Lori's great strides in doctrinal knowledge and spiritual understanding struck me. It was test time. When I made the test, I realized how many unfamiliar words and new concepts we had learned. At our previous lesson Lori had gritted her teeth and said, "tuff." She almost elided the *u* when she said the word, and it *really* sounded tough. Though we had laughed, she soberly promised she would study the lesson hard every evening. And here she was in class, easily underlining the answers in the red boxes and writing answers on the red lines, and feeling comfortable with *providence* and *omnipotence*.

As she worked through the paper, she gave me a quick, warm glance after each answer. On question 5 (see her worksheet) I raised my eyebrows at her answer, but she patted my arm as if I were a child who did not understand, and put the following scheme on the board:
     "God–) Jesus–) Lori–) Mrs. Hoekeman–) love God"
and she ran her finger in both directions on the line. Lori was explaining that our blessings come *through* Jesus, and all His blessings are *good;* and our love goes *back* to God through Jesus.

aust 8/1984

Lori

PRAYER

Today, O Father, as we pray to Thee, we thank Thee for Thy <u>providence</u>. We know that means that Thou wilt always take care of us, in Thy love. We thank Thee that we are Thy children who know that Thou dost make all things work for good for us who love God. Keep us from sinning against Thee, we pray, in Jesus' name. Amen

****

The first 5 questions are on Lesson 11

A

1. What is God's <u>providence</u>?   His

love for Jesus
~~taking care of us~~
making of the world

2. God is omnipresent. It means that

God is everywhere at the same time
God sleeps
God is very good

3. Does God rule the wicked people in His providence? ___Yes___

4. Does everything in the world happen just the way God wants it to happen? _Yes_

5. Does everything work together for good to them that love God? ___Jesus___

6. In Lesson 12 we learned that God is <u>eternal</u>. Eternal means that

God

is love
changes
always was and always will be

7. We learned that we are God's <u>adopted</u> children through <u>regeneration</u>.

Regeneration means that

we are sinners
we are born again
we are people

8. We know that Jesus is <u>one</u> person with <u>two</u> natures. Which are His two natures?

His

divine nature
human nature
old nature

(2 answers)

Does God ever change? ___no___

When at last, with wide and eloquent gestures, she had made me understand, with great ceremony I put another *A* on her finished paper.

But she was already pulling me up and telling me it was time to knock on the study door across the hall. As "Vite" studied her test, with Lori hanging on his arm, I knew we were both thinking how far the Lord had led Lori in a scant two years. Two years ago she was illiterate in Bible truths. Today she was at home with doctrinal terms, she understood them, and delighted in them.

The after-church-service coffee drinkers at Grandpa and Grandma Holstege were eager to see Lori's progress and to encourage her. She took her lessons to the coffee gathering, invited all the relatives to go over her papers with her, and basked in their praises. Lori still liked to be the center of attention.

She had her favorite concepts in each lesson. On August 15 our test was on the names and offices of our Mediator. When we came to question 6, she made sure I noticed the three times I had used the name of Christ (see her worksheet). And, predictably, she wrote on the chalkboard: "Love name Christian — Christ in Christian." These discoveries were like jewels to her.

In the next lesson we were studying the two states — *humiliation* and *exaltation* — of our Mediator. When I first taught Lori, in my wildest imagination, could I have thought that Lori would read and understand these terms with ease? I knew it now, and yet each new lesson I had taught Lori had its happy surprises. Sometimes her loving, sympathetic nature showed itself as she took her tests. When she answered question six, I pointed to *cried* and motioned surprise and asked why she had written that answer (see her worksheet).

Patiently she answered me: "Jesus feel bad — Lazarus die — cry". Then I remembered. Back in New Testament history, when we studied the story of Lazarus' death, Lori had wiped aust 22 1984

Lori

****

A

In lesson 15 we learned about the states of the Mediator, our Lord Jesus Christ. Remember, the <u>state</u> of Jesus was <u>what</u> happened to Him.

1. The two states of Jesus were
   His humiliation and exaltation
   His birth and His death
   His childhood and His growing up

2. What does <u>humiliation</u> means? Being very   low

3. What does <u>exaltation</u> mean? Being very   high

5. How many steps were there in Jesus' state of humiliation?   3   6   (5)

6. Can you tell me one <u>very low</u> thing that happened to Jesus on the earth? Cried-died

7. Can you tell me one <u>very high</u> thing that happened to Jesus? heaven

Lesson 16 was about the <u>Holy Ghost</u> or the <u>Holy Spirit</u>

8. Is the Holy Spirit God? yes

9. When was the Holy Spirit given to God's church on earth?
   On Christmas
   (On Pentecost)
   On Thanksgiving

10. Can you choose, Lori, of you own free will, whether you will believe in Jesus? no

****

Now 2 questions about the Bible story

. When Deborah and Barak fought God's emeny, God helped them by
   (making the river drown them)
   making the sun stand still
   (making the stars fall on them)   (2 answers)

What did Jael use to kill Sisera, the wicked captain?
   a spear
   a gun
   (a tent nail)

some tears, too. She felt so sorry for Jesus, especially because her enemies, the Pharisees, showed their hatred to her Lord. Now her feelings of sympathy came out in her test. She also felt sad because Jesus had to die such an awful death, and these impressions were permanently on her heart.

Lord's Day 33 asks: "Of how many parts doth the true conversion of man consist?" We read in our lesson that conversion happens *inside* one of God's children: it means that our old nature of sin dies in us, and the new life of Christ is born in us, and I pointed to her heart. I had much more to say, but Lori did not give me a chance.

She was suddenly so excited — making swings of her arm toward Hudsonville, peaking her hands for a church roof, holding one finger in the air and saying "one," and aiming totally disgusted sighs in my direction. I couldn't come close to guessing the cause for her excitement, so I motioned to calm down and write.

She wrote: "Rember (instead of remember — but something inside her was urgent) Matt. 3:17 — best in Holy Bible — Huds. church — lesson 1"

Yes, I remembered that lesson. How *could* I forget? We had started our lessons with the baptism of Jesus. But I did not see the connection, and Lori was quite unhappy with me.

I urged her to sit down. She did, and she started over with her explanation. She opened her Bible to Matthew 3:17, and began writing on the board: "Rember conversion — Huds. — Lesson 1— Jesus — beloved Son — God — Lori not know — then know."

She shared her Bible and we read the text together: "And lo a voice from heaven, saying, This is my beloved Son, in whom I am well pleased."

It all came clear to me. Lori dated her conversion from that first evening when she began to learn with her heart what salvation meant. It was no wonder that she was so excited by that text the first time we met together. God had spoken to her heart, and she would never forget the time when she first clearly understood that God came down from heaven to save us. Now she understood, too, for the first time, just what had happened to her that October evening in 1982. God had showed her His only begotten Son, and gave her grace to believe that He had come to save her. And now I, two years later, at last understood the reason for her excitement and joy in that particular text in Matthew 3. She dated her conversion and the knowledge of her salvation from it. No wonder it was such a favorite text!

* * * * * * * * * * * * * * * * * * *

In September we were racing the calendar to finish the study of the catechism. The date for her confession of faith was set for October 14, on her twenty-second birthday. Because she, too, would soon be allowed to take Lord's Supper, Lesson 21 was one of her favorites. I could not help thinking of the pathetic, desperate young girl, standing in the chill gloom of the narthex of Hudsonville Church, bewailing her life-long ignorance the first time she knew what the bread and the wine of the Lord's Supper symbolized. Neither of us could forget my promise that evening: that I would work hard to make her wish come true — her wish to be a confessing member of Christ's body, too. And here we were, learning all the doctrinal implications of the Lord's Supper, and fast reaching our goal for Lori to "embrace with a believing heart all the sufferings and death of Christ," Lord's Day 28.

She hardly seemed to be the same Lori, the Lori who now studied the concepts in depth. At test time she jostled my arm and laughed at my sometimes absurd multiple choices, but through it all she kept an earnestness to get every detail of the lesson perfect because it was for her spiritual welfare. It was hard for me to think of Lori as mentally handicapped.

* *

Because we had already studied God's law and the Lord's Prayer in detail in previous lessons, we only reviewed that part of the catechism, and were well able to finish the study of the Heidelberg by the beginning of October.

Pastor Gritters was arranging procedure for Lori's confession of faith before the consistory. The men knew well Lori's excellence in doctrinal knowledge. They had copies of all her lessons and worksheets. In view of that, the pastor suggested a simple, personal confession before the members of the council. The dear girl would be awed and nervous at the solemnity of the circumstances and occasion. By mid-September I wrote her:

> Lori, Rev. Gritters gave me some of the questions he will ask on the Wednesday night when you go to the consistory. I would like to go over them with you, to make sure you understand them. He told me he would not ask you the hard questions from the tests. The elders saw how well you did on the tests and they will not have to ask you *again.*
>
> The questions Rev. Gritters will ask are those that must be answered from your *heart.* You have to know and believe *in your heart* before you stand up in front of Byron Center Church. Do you understand?
>
> *
>
> Now I want to talk about something else. Eunice and I have a plan to do something nice for you. I would like to buy you some material for a suit and for a nice blouse to go with it — and that will be your birthday present and your Christmas present from me. Then Eunice will make the suit and blouse, and that will be her birthday and Christmas present to you. Would you like that for your birthday and Christmas presents?

After reading the first half of the paper, the part about appearing before the council, she was quiet, put her hand on my arm, and was a bit tearful. They *had* to be tears of joy, I told myself, as she picked up the chalk, carefully re-read the second paragraph, nodded, and wrote, "promise."

The next half of the note brought an entirely different reaction.

106

She bounded out of her chair, grabbed my arm, pulled me up, shouted her joy, and by the time she had finished expressing herself, we were almost dancing a jig. I had to concede, "Enough!" Truly, Lori dealt in absolutes: this time in total seriousness over the most important step in her life, and then in total frivolity over a new outfit.

The outfit Lori chose was a suit in a soft plaid in shades of blues and creamy whites, with a blue blouse trimmed with narrow ivory lace — a striking outfit in beautiful taste.

What is your only comfort in life and in death?

That I am not my own, but belong — body and soul, in life and in death —
to my faithful Savior

JESUS CHRIST.

He has fully paid for all my sins with his precious blood and has set me free from the
tyranny of the devil. He also watches over me in such a way that not a hair
can fall from my head without the will of my

HEAVENLY FATHER.

In fact, all things must work together for my salvation.
Because I belong to him, Christ, by his

HOLY SPIRIT

assures me of eternal life and makes me wholeheartedly willing and ready
from now on to live for him.

_____ LORI JO HOLSTEGE _____

born __October 14__, 19 _62_, *a baptized member of the church of Christ has publicly made*

Profession of Faith on Sunday __October 14__, 19 _84_, *in the* __Protestant Reformed__

Church, __Byron Center, Michigan__, *and is now welcome to full communion with the people of God.*

Pastor _Rev. Barry Gritters_ ____ *Clerk* _Sid. Meedema_

108

Chapter 9

Lori's Confession

Our lessons in Room 3 of Hudsonville Church were over. From the fall of 1984 onward, we had lessons in my office. The transportation was easier, and Lori liked it better. Lori, heavy-footed and uncoordinated, had a lilt in her steps these days as she bounced into the house, usually in mid-sentence. She had started her sentence, of course, the moment she had stepped from the car. Usually she made straight for the note pad, and we chatted about the progress of the new outfit, her classmates from Kent Occupational High School who were coming to church for her confession of faith on October 14, the plans for refreshments afterwards — and maybe presents. It would be her birthday, too! Excitement was at an all-time high!

Her appearance to make confession of faith before the consistory was scheduled for Wednesday, October 3. We arranged that she would come for a short briefing on the procedures and the questions for that evening immediately after school on Wednesday afternoon. Then she would rest, to be fresh and ready with a clear mind to answer the questions that evening. We had both agreed that we wanted everything to be perfect.

But both Lori and I learned that nothing in this life is perfect, and that in spite of all our planning, our Father sometimes says that circumstances less than perfect are best for us. That afternoon Lori did something she had never before done. With the look of thunder clouds on her face, she stepped from her mother's car. She stamped into the house, banged the door, and shouted at me. Lori had never done that!

I went for the note pad, and scribbled, "Lori, you may *never* come into this house mad and shouting. Very wrong. Calm down."

By the time the note was written, she was standing quietly next to me, her head down, crying. It might be best to go downstairs, where we could communicate better. Without the lilt, Lori's heavy steps went down to my office, and my heavy heart followed. We sat down. Slowly the story came out, with motions and with words on the chalkboard. When mother had taken her to this lesson, she had suggested that Lori go to the Friendship meeting with other handicapped children at another church that evening, and have the Byron Center consistory meeting, where Lori was to confess her faith that evening, changed to another date. Lori enjoyed the Friendship meetings, and was usually eager to go. At the same time, she had been working hard to reach this climax of the expression of her faith. Lori was confused and upset.

I asked, "What do you think?"

She shrugged her shoulders and sat glumly looking at the floor.

After a while she wrote, "Both important."

"Lori, did we work for two years to teach you the fear and love of the Lord? Did we work hard to get you ready to confess your faith?"

She nodded.

"Is confessing that you belong to Jesus the most important thing you can do in your life?"

She nodded again, with a pathetic face.

"Do you know what you should do tonight?"

She wrote "no" on the board. I scrutinized her face. Her jaw was set. Her eyes were stony. Was she being stubborn? No, it was not the face of a stubborn girl. There was fear in her face, too. She was troubled and confused and pressured and did not know what to do.

It was best, then, to do nothing about it right now. When she had been troubled in the past, the lesson — no matter on what

110

aspect of Scripture it was centered — had spoken to her, and had taken her doubts and troubles away. Maybe the Lord would use the last review of her questions for her confession to speak to her.

I smiled at her, even though my sinking heart hardly allowed me to. As we rather dubiously started our review of the procedure and the questions Pastor Gritters had prepared, Lori was not giving her full attention. Churning inside, but trying to exude encouragement, I stroked Lori's arm instead of Lori stroking mine. If only she could quiet down!

As we went through the list of questions in the first group, I thought I could feel her relax slightly. Was it my imagination? She still responded only half-heartedly.

When we came to the second group, which addressed her personal life and walk, she perked up a little, and I thought I could see my real Lori emerging again. Slowly, and a bit sluggishly, she motioned for a halt, picked up the chalk, and wrote, "Know now — Byron Center — 8 p.m."

The miracle had happened! Lori could not set aside the importance of her personal confession with its seriousness and its implications for the rest of her life on earth and for her life with Jesus forever. No, that was not quite right. The Lord had touched her heart through the words of those questions, and showed her that the way of the confession of her faith was the right way and the only way. In what I did next, our roles were reversed. I was the one, instead of Lori, who wrote, "Thank the Lord!"

As she left, she told me she had one more worry: she wanted to wear a nice dress tonight, and there was no time to go to father's house and get one. I had noticed that Lori, who usually was very well groomed, did not look her best today. She was not dressed for a meeting.

"Slacks and a neat blouse?" I suggested.

She shrugged as if second best would have to do; and she left more despondent than I had ever seen my Lori — on the evening of what was to be the climax, the crowning joy of her long and steady growth to spiritual maturity, and the night of the most memorable step she would ever take.

Lori, her father, and I met in the hall of Byron Center Christian Junior High School, where the consistory was meeting in one of the rooms. The first question my demure Lori asked me (by motion) was, "Do I look all right?" Her neat blouse and slacks were fine, her hair carefully done, and her face was lovely. How could I ever have thought that Lori wasn't beautiful? It probably wasn't her physical features. I think it was her soul shining through.

Almost immediately we were called into the room with Pastor Gritters and the elders, and he handed us a sheet with questions, which we had already studied — or tried to — that afternoon. Pastor Gritters read the first part to us all:

> Lori, we are *very glad* that you are here. We know how much *you* want to make confession. And *we* want you to confess your faith, too. We are glad that your father could come here with you. We know that this is a special time for him too. He loves you and is happy to see you come here.
>
> We are glad that Mrs. Hoeksema could come here. This is a very special time for her.
>
> So your father is here, and Mrs. Hoeksema is here, and we are here — the consistory. We all love you and want you to feel *relaxed.*
>
> We are *not* going to fool you. We are elders and deacons because Jesus Christ called us to do this work. And the love of Jesus Christ rules this consistory.
>
> So *please* don't be afraid. Feel free here.

Lori and I had planned a surprise. Only her pastor was in on it with us, and it had been Lori's idea. Because she *loved* the first question and answer of the Heidelberg Catechism, she had memorized the first part of the answer in her bedroom, before she went to sleep, she told me. Might she say it for the elders? What a great idea! We practiced it with Lori saying the answer by herself and Lori saying it following my lips. She tended to have less precise speech when she did not watch my lips, but she liked the idea of saying it independently, too. I gave her the choice. In the end, she chose to follow my lips.

This is what Pastor Gritters said next:
"These are the questions we would like you to answer.
After I ask each question, *please look at me and answer.*
* *

LORI, WHAT IS YOUR ONLY COMFORT IN LIFE AND DEATH?
(you may look at Mrs. Hoeksema for this question)"

Our eraser followed his words, and when she had read the question, she looked at me, took a deep breath, and distinctly and slowly said, "That I belong to my faithful Savior, Jesus Christ." It was a complete surprise and a beautiful confession, and Lori's father and some of the elders shed tears.

The questions for Lori, following the order of the questions for public confession of faith, were divided into three groups. The first group, asking her to confess that the doctrine she had learned and believed was the perfect doctrine of salvation, she answered with confident yesses and nos.

I. FIRST GROUP
1. Lori, do you believe that *the Bible is God's Word?* "Yes."
2. Do you think that *the Bible has any mistakes?* "No"
3. Do you believe that *the Bible has all you need to know about God?* "Yes"
4. Do you believe that *the APOSTLES' CREED teaches what the Bible says?* "Yes"
5. Do you believe that *OUR CHURCHES teach what the Bible teaches?* "Yes "
6. Do you believe that *God loves ONLY His people?* "Yes"
7. Do you think that God loves *all* men? "No"

Then followed the second group, the part that asked her about her personal salvation, and Pastor Gritters read:

"1. Lori, Have you *decided to keep the truths of the Bible in your heart?*" Lori answered, "Yes."

Underneath came a sub-question: "Can you do that by yourself?" Again Lori answered, "Yes." Pastor Gritters motioned for me to tell her to try that one again. I ran my pencil over it, and this time she said "Yes" more emphatically. Suddenly I knew what Lori was thinking. I said, "Go on to the next question and I think Lori's problem will be solved." So we read, "Do you think that *only* God can help you do that?" and without answering, she clapped her hand over her mouth and said, "Oh!" and smiled at Pastor Gritters and went into a quick explanation of her misunderstanding, with words and gestures: "Can I myself do it? Yes, I can!"

She had omitted the word *by* and interpreted, "Can you yourself make this confession?"

With another smile at her pastor, she gave a resounding "No," and went on to answer the rest of the questions, while the ripple of laughter died down in the room. Poor Lori! Always getting tangled up in the meaning of the written word!

She breezed through the rest of the questions:

2. Do you promise *to fight against all lies about the Bible?* "Yes"
3. Do you promise *to live like a Christian?* "Yes"
4. Do you promise *to live different* than how you used to live? "Yes"

III. THIRD GROUP

1. God gives elders and ministers to rule the church in the name of Christ. Do you promise *to obey* when they bring God's Word to you? "Yes"

2. If you sin, Lori, and *don't* ask for forgiveness, God says the elders must come to visit you with God's Word. We pray to God that will not happen, Lori. But will you obey them if they *must* come to you? "Yes"

After answering these questions, Lori read on her paper: "Lori, please go out of the room for a few minutes. We will vote to see if you may make confession of faith before the whole church. We will call you back after we vote."

Lori, her father, and I left the room. It took us a long time out in the hall to finish all our hugs for Lori and tell each other our happiness. All too soon Pastor Gritters called us in and gave Lori another sheet.

Lori, we have voted to let you make confession of faith. We believe that God has worked faith in your heart. And you showed that to us tonight.

God does good things for us. All that you did tonight was *HIS WORK in you.* We must thank God for all that we are. (When you go home tonight, look in *The Psalter* at number 383 — the first verse. It says: "All that I am I owe to Thee. . . .")

We are *very happy* for you! We are happy, because we know God wants us to make confession of faith. And we are happy because we know you are happy.

We decided that *you will make confession in church* on
OCTOBER 14, IN THE EVENING SERVICE
We would like to congratulate you now, Lori. The consistory will shake your hand. After that we will pray together.
* *
PRAYER: Father in heaven, we thank *Thee.* We thank Thee for this wonderful work in Lori's heart. We know that *we* cannot do anything apart from THEE. All our strength is in THEE.

We thank Thee for the Bible. It tells us all about THEE, and about Jesus Christ. Thy Word is precious to us.

We thank Thee for Mrs. Hoeksema, who taught Lori so much from the Bible. Lori has learned the truth of salvation by grace, in Jesus' blood. She has learned that we cannot save ourselves. Our salvation is *all* from Thee. We thank Thee for Mrs. Hoeksema's many hours of work with Lori.

And we thank Thee for Lori's father, who is here as a witness of his love for his daughter, and for the truth of Thy Word. We thank Thee that he can continue in this work of teaching his covenant children. We know that his task is difficult, without his wife. So we pray for strength for him. Bless him, Father. Give him the grace necessary for his work in his home.

God, grant us all to make our calling and election sure. Give us the strength to live a new and godly life, as we all have promised. So bless us by Thy grace and Spirit.

Help Lori to make this confession every day of her life: "My only comfort in life and death is that I, with body and soul, both in life and death, am not my own, but belong unto my faithful Savior Jesus Christ."

Help Lori to *live* her confession.

And help her to be strong, so in a few weeks she can stand before the church, and confess her faith there.

Forgive our sins, Father. We are sinful. We have sinned even in this short time. Forgive us in Jesus' blood.

We pray this in His name, AMEN.

* *

Thank you for coming, Lori. We are very happy for you tonight. Congratulations, again. Good-bye.

After the prayer, three happy people went home.

* * * * * * * * * * * * * * * * * * * *

On Saturday the thirteenth, Eunice and Lori exchanged notes about the next evening. Eunice wrote: "I finished all the pieces of your outfit. You can wear the two plaid pieces together. In chilly weather you can wear the blue blouse under the plaid one. Leave the top button of the plaid top open then. Or you can wear the blue blouse and the tie. Remember not to use a *hot iron* on these clothes. Did you get new shoes, too?

"The boys made you something special for your celebration tomorrow night. They made candy mints and want you to set them out with refreshments after church. Don't you think they are pretty? They are good, too. Don't eat them all before Oct. 14!!!

"After all the excitement of your birthday and making con-fession of faith is over, would you like to make a Christmas gift for Aunt Marcia? She helps you very much in church and you can thank her by making her a nice gift. I have stuff to make beautiful placemats for her table. If you want to do this, I will show you how to make them.

116

"Get Debbie to tie a nice bow in your blouse tomorrow."

Lori responded to Eunice's "mother-hen" type note: "Tomorrow Sunday — Oct. 14 — I will go to church — blouse — suit blue."

Eunice had the last word: "Do not wear it in the morning. Skirt gets messy."

Lori ranked Sunday, October 14, 1984, as the best day of her life. When we — her teacher, pastor, family, and friends — considered that a profoundly deaf girl with scarcely any speech, and somewhat mentally handicapped, now knew most of Bible history and had learned the doctrines of the church, delving far deeper than many young people her age, we knew it was a miracle of grace.

Now the logistics of having a deaf girl make confession of faith in a congregation of hearing people were yet to be solved. The week before Sunday, the 14th, Lori had gone over the order of the evening service and her part in it. Pastor Gritters had produced a whole worship for Lori, with her part in it clearly defined, including the questions he would ask her, his little talk to her after the questions, a special prayer with which he would start his congregational prayer, and an outline of his sermon for the occasion. We were ready.

The gym-turned-auditorium of the Christian Junior High School was packed with people: besides the members of the congregation of Byron Center were relatives, friends from the Hudsonville congregation (Lori's former church home), her friends from school, her handicapped friends (with whom she still had craft parties), and their families. Lori, pretty in her new outfit, attractive with modest make-up, quiet and sober, yet seething with the joy and excitement of the evening, walked into the auditorium with me and followed me to the front row.

Before the service started, she was concerned about the "Yes" she would answer to the questions asked her. We had practiced almost endlessly, at Lori's insistence, at our last lesson. She was so worried that it would not be loud and clear enough. She told me that she and father had practiced it again at home many times, and she opened her mouth and pantomimed her *yes* for me, cupping her mouth with her hands and using her whole body in the effort. I told her I felt sure it would be perfect, and because I did not want her to dwell on it, I changed the subject. I told her that our minister in Hudsonville had prayed for her in the morning service, and her look of love and joy told me what was in her heart. Then the service began.

When Pastor Gritters asked her to rise after we had sung the second song, she was more relaxed than I was. We stood together and followed on our paper the three questions he asked her:

1. Do you acknowledge the doctrine contained in the Old and New Testaments and in the Articles of the Christian faith and taught here in this Christian church to be the true and complete doctrine of salvation?

2. Have you resolved by the grace of God to adhere to this doctrine; to reject all heresies repugnant thereto and to lead a new, godly life?

3. Will you submit to church government, and in case you should become delinquent (which may God graciously forbid) to church discipline?

Lori moved to the rhythm of the words which the eraser of the pencil followed, nudging me and nodding her head to let me know that she understood those big words we had studied, completely forgetful of the congregation behind us. When Pastor Gritters asked, "What is your answer, Lori?" she said, loudly, "Ye-es-sa!" It resounded to the back of the auditorium. Then utterly uninhibited, she cocked her head at me to get my approval.

I gave her a quick rub of her arm, for Pastor Gritters was ready to address her in a little talk. We remained standing and followed on our paper. He started with, "Lori, your church, your family, and your friends, rejoice in your confession of faith."

The pastor went on: "We rejoice because God has worked in your heart. You wanted to stand before the church of Jesus Christ, and confess that Jesus Christ is *your* Lord. And that confession you made is the fruit of God's work in your heart. We thank God for that.

"It makes God's people rejoice when they see young men and women of the church make confession of faith. We see the fruit of God's grace in the lines of the covenant.

"This is *the first confession of faith* that we have had in Byron Center congregation. And I think it is one that we will not forget, either. This is *special* for us here."

Lori poked me, smiled (in her way) at me and then at her pastor. It was delightful to her, but I heard sniffles behind us.

We read on: "It is *special*, too, because God has worked faith in your heart. You are not able to hear. Yet God has made you hear the gospel of Jesus Christ in your heart. You are not able to speak, but God has given you the power and the desire to confess your faith. God has limited the power of your mind, yet we know that He has given you the ability to understand the heart of the gospel — that Jesus Christ died for sinners, 'of whom I am the chief!!' And though none of us here is able to believe, yet God, by the power of His Spirit, has taken out our hearts of stone, and given us hearts of flesh — hearts that can believe.

"That is what we thank God for. We thank Him for the *wonder of grace* in your life."

Then we read, "Lori, you may sit down now."

Pastor Gritters had made a prayer thanking God for Lori's confession, which he read as the first part of his congregational prayer. Lori and I followed the prayer with the ever-present eraser:

"Lord God in heaven, we confess that Thy name is great, and greatly to be praised. Thou art Jehovah, our covenant God, faithful and true to us. And through Jesus Christ our Lord Thy covenant has been established with us and our children.

"Thou art faithful to Thy covenant children, in giving them the power of faith in their hearts. Thou art faithful in giving to us children who believe in Thee, and in the Lord Jesus Christ Whom Thou has sent. We thank Thee for the blessings of Thy covenant. We see the fruit of Thy blessings in our children. And especially we see the fruit of Thy Spirit in this confession tonight.

"Lord, we thank Thee, too, for this marvelous confession of faith. It is a testimony of the power of Thy grace in Lori's heart. We know that she could never have done that by herself, but only by Thy Spirit in her heart."

While the rest of the congregation sat with closed eyes and bowed heads, Pastor Gritters, Lori, and I were reading the prayer. As the pastor gave us a quick glance, Lori looked up, caught his eye, and gave him another of her unique, sincere smiles. It was a first confession of faith for him as pastor, a first and only time he would have a Lori sitting in the front row, and I wondered whether her spontaneity threw him a bit off guard.

When he finished the special part of the prayer for Lori, Pastor Gritters went into the congregational prayer, while Lori read a special prayer I had prepared for her.

Pastor Gritters had not told Lori ahead of time what the text for the sermon would be. After the prayer and a song, he asked us to turn to Romans 10. He read the chapter for the congregation, and Lori and I followed in her Bible. We came to verse 9

120

and she gasped, clapped her hand over her mouth, and motioned, "Is this it?" She had guessed right. The sermon he was to preach (and of which she had a resume) was based on Romans 10:9, 10: "That if thou shalt confess with thy mouth the Lord Jesus, and shalt believe in thine heart that God hath raised him from the dead, thou shalt be saved. For with the heart man believeth unto righteousness; and with the mouth confession is made unto salvation."

In part, Lori's sermon read:

> WE MUST CONFESS OUR FAITH.
> First, that means that we *speak what we believe.*
> You confess your faith when you say "yes" to these questions. You confess your faith when you *tell* Mrs. H. or your father that you love God. You confess your faith when you *say* that you are sorry for your sins. You confess your faith when you *pray!*
> But you also confess your faith *in your life.* How do you *live?* Do you *live* like you are one of God's people? Do you *dress* like one of God's people? That is confessing your faith, too. . . .
> Second, confessing our faith means that *we say the same thing.* When you stood up here tonight, you said the same thing that all the rest of the church says. You did not stand alone tonight. The whole church of Byron Center is with you. And you say just what the church confesses. We say that together. That is what confess means. WE SPEAK TOGETHER!!
>
> WHEN WE BELIEVE AND CONFESS, *WE WILL BE SAVED!*
> Now you have made confession of faith, Lori. And now you may come to the table of the Lord. You may celebrate communion with the rest of God's people. You may eat the bread and drink the wine that we pass. . . . And when we eat and drink the Lord's body and blood, God makes us *know* that we are saved!

Childlike, and yet mature as she read the sermon and filled in the blanks Pastor Gritters had left for her, she bothered me a lot, just to share her joy; and tonight she might bother me as much as she wanted to!

After the service, Lori and I went to the back of the auditorium for Lori to receive congratulations, cards, and gifts, not only for her confession of faith, but for her birthday, too. We all stayed for refreshments, and Lori was truly the guest of honor — so much so that she lagged, and father had to take her aside to give her an insulin shot.

And a radiant Lori told me before we went home that it was the most important and best day of her life. She always carried her copy of the service in her notebook. She told me, too, that she often read it at bedtime; and occasionally we would go over it again together. It was too precious to forget.

Chapter 10

Lori Matures

Lori had climbed to the heights! By God's grace and through His strength she had learned in two years what most covenant young people learn gradually and more casually through a lifetime of Christian instruction. She had climbed a mountain of instruction, and on October 14, 1984, had stood on the peak, when she made her confession. Very soon, in unity with the rest of the body of Christ, she would take the Lord's Supper.

Would she think she had arrived? That she was finished learning? That anything else would be anti-climactic? I would soon know.

I suggested a little time off after the fast pace and the excitement of the last few months, but Lori was not happy when she could not come to her lessons. She told Eunice at church to tell her mother that it was time we take up our work again. So we did!

There were three areas in which Lori needed help and instruction. The first had to do with her godly walk. How does God's Word teach her to *live* and to *act* and to *think*? What does God teach her about the way she acts toward her friends, her fellow Christians? Although Lori was a friend to all, she had never had specific training in proper behavior toward family and friends *for God's sake.* Yes, she told me, she would like me to teach her about *that*!

One of the lessons was titled: "This is Something To Think About;" and it was a talk with Lori about *why* she was called to do the unpleasant things in life, for God's sake. I wrote, in part:

> Lori, I want to talk with you about *work.* You are a Christian young girl, and I do not think you understand how you must think about *work.* Because I am your teacher, I will tell you about it.
> Do you want to know what *God* says about it? He says that He put us on this earth to work: to take care of His world, to get food from it, to build houses on it, and to take care of each other on it.
> Not all work is fun. Sometimes we get very dirty. Sometimes we

get our clothes dirty. Or we get tired or hot or thirsty or grumpy. And then we get mad and say we do not want to work. We even say bad words to father and mother and say NO to them. This is a very bad sin.

Do you know what God thinks about that? *God* is the One Who tells us to work and God is the One Who tells us to obey our father and mother, and it is a very bad sin to say NO to God.

I could tell that Lori had matured. She was not erupting so vigorously as she had in earlier lessons. In this lesson, where the material concerned her own way of life, she had a solemn look on her face, pointed her finger at herself, and told me candidly that she was surely guilty of the negative attitudes I had described.

Now that she understood her faults, I wanted her to know the *two reasons why* she should obey her parents willingly. The first one was:

"God gave you a nice, strong body, Lori, and He wants you to use it in love to Him. And even when you think you do not feel like working, you make yourself happy for *God's sake;* and you get dirty and tired because *God* calls you to work. God wants you to change yourself from the inside and He wants you to go to work with a smile. Then you will work because you love God."

The second reason was:

"God wants you to work because you love your family and your friends, and you show your love by working hard for them. Then you forget all about yourself. You love your family so much that you forget all the bad parts of work and you do what they say with a happy face. Do you think you can work for father and mother with a happy face? Remember, you do this because God puts *His* love in your heart."

Lori agreed. But more was coming. She needed a reproof, and she had it in the next paragraph:

124

"On Wednesday I saw a mad Lori shout at mother because she did not want to work. That was a sin, and God hates it. Will you tell God you are sorry, and promise to try from now on to work with a happy face and a happy heart? If you have trouble being happy while you work, just pray to God and ask Him to help you be a good, obedient, loving girl who will do what He wants."

It was seldom that Lori had a scolding from me, and she accepted it quietly. Would she take it to heart?

Shortly afterward her father asked me, "What did you teach Lori, anyway? She would *never* work in the muck, and last week she did. She doesn't like work, period. Now she's doing some things in the house willingly."

Lori was like all of us. She was not perfect. She had her ups and downs with willingness to work, but she was God's child, and by His grace she fought her faults. She still gave her family problems at times, but she knew better now, and she tried harder, and she was sorry when she sinned. She was trying to live her confession.

In January of 1985, Lori had another exciting "first" in her life. She was a bridesmaid at her sister Debbie's wedding.

Meanwhile, the lessons went on. During this 1984-85 lesson season, Pastor Gritters suggested alternating lesson times with me. He wanted to get more accustomed to communicating with her, and besides, he was very fond of her, as everyone else was. As a result, I taught Lori only every other week. Her pastor gave her special instruction on the sermons he wrote for her for worship services and taught her much about the art of prayer, particularly the three proper elements of prayer: the elements of petition, of praise, and of thanks.

After Lori learned what it meant to be godly in a few more areas of Christian living, we moved on to the second area I had in mind to teach her: the psalms and their relationship to the songs in the Psalter. I still sat with Lori in church occasionally, whenever circumstances allowed me to go to Byron Center, and I noticed that her participation in the songs was lagging. Poor girl! I could understand! Would *I* like to lip words and try a rhythm in complete silence? But the words were so beautiful and would help Lori so much in her spiritual growth. If she *knew* more about them she would love them more, and try to sing them better.

I also wanted to find out if she understood that our songs were rhymed versions, taken from the psalms.

In our first lesson on the psalms, I wrote:

"Lori, do you remember I gave you a paper about the psalms to work on in church? We say *psalms* this way: *sahms*. For a few weeks, I would like to have you learn about the psalms.

"Psalms are *songs* and *prayers*. Some are long. Some are short. David, the king of Israel, wrote many of them. The people of Israel in the land of Canaan long ago sang them and prayed them. We who live in the United States still sing and pray them. All God's children love the psalms."

Lori liked David, the shepherd boy and the king. When she read his name, she picked up the chalk, sketched a free-hand map of Palestine, locating Jerusalem, where David ruled as king, and let me know what she meant by placing an imaginary crown on her head. That being finished, she came right back to the lesson — until she came to the words *United States.* Under the words she drew a map and labelled it "Michigan," and then the word "airplane," and indicated the ways we could fly from Michigan to parts of the United States, listing her favorites on the board: Chicago, Florida, Sandusky, Ohio. . . .

Yet it did not seem to distract us. As if maps and airplanes were not unusual in a lesson on the psalms, Lori matter-of-factly read on:

126

"You will like to know what many of the psalms talk about:

1. about the difference between God's people and wicked people
2. about how bad our sins are and how God washes us clean from them
3. about how much we love God's Word, the Bible
4. about how happy we are because we have our God to take care of us
5. about how *great* God is and how *little* we are.

"We will find psalms that tell about these five things. Find Psalm 1. You looked at this one in church, too. Remember? Read verse 1. Lori read: 'Blessed is the man that walketh not in the counsel of the ungodly, nor standeth in the way of sinners, nor sitteth in the seat of the scornful.'

"The *counsel of the ungodly* are the *words of the wicked people. Scornful* is a man who makes fun of God with a bad heart. Verse 1 tells about wicked men. Verse 2 tells what God's children do. Read it." Lori read: "But his delight is in the law of the Lord, and in his law doth he meditate day and night.

"*Meditate* means to *think.* We like to think about God's law and God's Word in the day and in the night — before we go to sleep in bed. . . ."

After I explained each verse of the psalm, we explored the psalm's versification. Lori read:

"Then some of God's people made *songs,* with music, from the psalms. They had to change the words a little bit to fit the tune of the music. Lori, you have never heard music. But you already know that when we sing songs in church, we make our voices go higher and lower. Let's look at Psalter number 1. Some of the notes are quick and some we hold with our voices for a little longer time. You already know that is why I tap out the rhythm for you when we sing in church. Music is very beautiful, Lori.

You will love it when you get to heaven and hear God's people and the angels sing.

"When God's people made the songs, they changed some of the words to make them *rhyme*. Do you know what *rhyme* means? The words *end* the same, and that makes them sound the same: like *cat* and *hat*. Now look at Psalter number 1 and find the words that rhyme."

We read the first stanza:
    That man is blest who, fearing God,
    From sin restrains his feet,
    Who will not stand with wicked men,
    Who shuns the scorner's seat.

And Lori, like a young child, enjoyed finding and underlining *feet* and *seat*.

We ended the lesson with a bit of a practical application. Lori still needed that:

"Do you want to know why I am teaching you the psalms, Lori? Because, when we read the psalms and sing the songs in church, we are doing it *to God*!

"Sometimes you look around in church instead of singing. I know it is hard for you to sing when you cannot hear the music, but it is wrong to look around. You can *see* when the notes go high and low and fast and slow, and you can try to hear it in your mind. And you will *love* the words."

As soon as the lesson was over, this irrepressible girl told me that she *liked* this lesson, and that she was going to spend *two hours* in her room at bedtime, finding more rhymes and the fast and slow notes in the Psalter.

As we studied other psalms, Lori showed me which ones she had chosen to read on her own. That reassured me. For before I started the psalms with her, I had some doubts. Lori liked vibrant, action-filled Bible history. And the psalms were meditative. What had I forgotten? That they would appeal to Lori's poetic soul, of course.

We studied several more psalms, among them Psalms 23, 34, 51. . . , but she seemed to favor Psalm 139. She *loved* to know more about God's care and presence, and she made motions of God's arms around her as we read about all the areas in which God's hand was over us and His eyes watching us, in verse 2: "Thou knowest my downsitting and mine uprising. . ." and in verse 5: "Thou hast beset me behind and before, and laid thine hand upon me." I asked myself a question: does a girl as handicapped as Lori feel the need for her Father's care, and experience His care in a more striking way and in richer measure than we who have no serious handicaps? I think so.

These are a few paragraphs from the lesson on Psalm 139, with Lori's responses:

"First we will look at Psalm 139, Lori. David wrote it. After you read it, it may be your favorite psalm! The Bible tells us that God is everywhere. We can *never* get away from God. Does that make you afraid?" Lori answered "No." We went on: "God loves His children so much that we do not *want* to get away from Him. We want Him to stay close to us to take care of us.

"When we read the psalm together, I will ask you to find some answers from the Bible. You will like to do that.

"In verse 1, *searched* means *looked into*. Now read verse 2. God knows when we sit *down* and when we get *up*. What else in this verse does God understand?" Lori wrote, "thought."

We stopped there and I asked, "Do you like it that God knows your thoughts?"

The expression on her face told me that she knew it was a loaded question, and she answered it as such on the board: "yes and no," graphically demonstrated examples — solemn prayer for the yes; and getting angry with Tracy for the no. And when she finished her illustrations, she answered my original question, when I repeated it, with a serious yes.

Once more I wanted the Scripture to speak to her handicap, through David's words in this psalm, in verses 13 and 14: "For thou hast possessed my reins: thou hast covered me in my mother's womb. I will praise thee; for I am fearfully and wonderfully made: marvellous are thy works. . . ."

But Lori beat me to it. My lover of babies and expert on the next census started listing all her acquaintances who were to have babies in the near future, and guessed whether they would have boys or girls, and we spent a little time on her list on the board.

The digression being over, we read in our lesson: "Verses 13 and 14 tell us that the Lord took care of you even before you were born. He *made* you. He even made you *deaf.* And that was good!" She thought, and said "um-m," and her face told me that if God made her deaf, then it wasn't so bad.

After we finished the psalm, we compared it with the versifications in the Psalter. She immediately favored the second stanza of number 383, marked it on her paper, and told me she wanted to copy it before she went to bed. This is the stanza Lori liked:

> Ere into being I was brought,
> Thy eye did see, and in Thy thought
> My life in all its perfect plan
> Was ordered ere my days began.

For my Lori, lover of God's works in nature, I chose parts of Psalm 147 and 148 so that she would grow in appreciation of His wonders in the world He created. We went through these psalms looking specifically for His wonders in nature. In Psalm

147 we found: the heavens covered with clouds, grass growing on the mountains, the beast getting his food, the strength of the horse, the snow and ice and cold.

Psalm 148 was more exciting to Lori. She found: angels, sun, moon, and stars, fire, hail, stormy winds, trees, beasts, cattle, creeping things and flying fowl.

Suddenly we had an uproar only a little less violent than the one we had when Lori first learned the creation story. All these wonders in nature were too much for her to take in all at once. She was standing next to me by this time, describing them, acting out her reactions, when, without ceremony, she picked up her lesson sheet and took off for the study. She remembered to knock, and went in to share with "Vite."

Rather exhausted — for lessons with Lori were often tiring — I stayed in my office to straighten some of the materials my young cyclone had scattered, and then followed her into the study. It was rather quiet again, and "Vite" and Lori were reading verse 2 of Psalm 148: "Praise ye him, all his angels: praise him all his hosts," and Lori was explaining to him that *that* was what she was eager for: to see the angels when she went to heaven.

* * * * * * * * * * * * * * * * * * * *

While we went on with our lessons that season, learning the wonder of God's Word, Lori's church life was also being enriched. On December 9, 1984, Lori took Lord's Supper in the communion of saints in Byron Center Church for the first time. Pastor Gritters furnished Lori with an abbreviated version of his sermon, as usual:

> Lori, this is God's Word that I am bringing to the church this morning. Please read and copy the Bible verses. Then read this paper, two times.
>
> Romans 12:4, 5
>
> (Lori copied the words: "For as we have many members in one body, and all members have not the same office: so we, being many,

are one body in Christ, and everyone members one of another.")

Lori, these verses from the Bible tell us about *communion*. Communion is the same as *The Lord's Supper*. When we have the Lord's Supper this morning with the bread and the wine, we *commune* with each other and with God.

The Lord's Supper = Communion

Communion = visiting, speaking, loving, friends

That is what we do this morning. We do that with God. We do that with others from church.

* *

The verse from Romans talks about your body. The church is like that body.

1. You have *many parts* to your body. You have arms and legs, hands and feet, fingers and toes, eyes and ears, nose and hair — many parts in your body. *That is like the church.* There are many members in the church of Jesus. Can you count all the people in the church? No. There are more than you can count.

2. All the parts of your body *are different*, too. Your arms are different from your legs. Your eyes are not the same as your ears. And your feet are different from your hands. Even your two hands are not the same. *That is like the church, too.* All the people in the church are different, too. You are different from me. Marcia is not the same as Mrs. Hoeksema. Tracy is different from Deb.

3. The parts of your body need your head, don't they? If you did not have a head, your arms couldn't do anything. If your head was gone, your feet would not know where to take you. You need your head for the rest of your body. Your body needs to be connected to your head. If you cut off your ear from your head, the ear can't hear. *The church is like that, too.* Jesus Christ is the head of the church. The church has parts just like your body. And if you are cut off from Christ, you can't do anything.

* *

But, Lori, you also need the other members of the church.

Your hand can't say to your arm, "I don't need you." What would your hands do without your arm? Or what would your feet do without your legs? Can your feet say, "I don't need my legs?" No. All the parts of the body need the other part. *The church is like that, too.* All the people need the other people. Lori, I need you. You need Marcia. Marcia needs others in the church. We all need each other. I can't say, "I don't need you." That would be like the foot saying to the leg, "I don't need you."

* *

Why is this true?

1. **We** are members of Christ's body because He died for us. Christ makes **us** part of His body by His blood. He paid for our sins. And now God gives us *faith* to make us part of Christ. And now we have the life of Christ in our hearts.

2. **That** is why we need each other. God gave us the life of Christ in our hearts. And that life looks for others who have the same kind of life. When we love God, we look for friends who love God, too. We **want** to "commune" with each other. We want to be friends with God's **friends**. We want to visit with God's friends. We want to be with God's friends.

* *

There is a picture of that in the Lord's Supper!!

1. **When** we eat the bread and drink the wine, God shows us that we **eat and** drink Christ! God feeds us with the food we *can* see — bread **and** wine. God feeds us with food we *can't* see — Jesus Christ. *The bread* is a picture of Jesus' body — it was broken on the cross. *The wine* is a picture of Jesus' blood — it was poured out on the cross.

2. And when you eat with all the others in Christ, Lori, it is a picture of our communion with each other. We eat the same bread. **We drink the** same wine. We eat at the same time. We drink at the **same time.** We eat and drink next to each other. We are friends with each other. We are friends with God.

Prayer: Father in heaven, we thank Thee for Jesus Christ. We thank Thee for friends in church. We thank Thee that Jesus died on the cross for us. And broke His body and poured out His blood *for our sins.* Feed us by Jesus' body and blood in our hearts.

For Jesus' sake, AMEN.

All her friends knew how eager Lori was to partake of the visible signs and seals of the body of Christ. Lori and I knew it even more acutely, with our poignant memories of that bleak evening in the darkness of Hudsonville Church we could not forget, when she begged to be a full and mature member of Christ's body. Lori understood what she was about to do. She had read the beautiful words of the sermon her pastor had prepared. But it was such a new experience, crowding in on so many other new and exciting happenings, that she was hesitant at first, flustered and self-conscious; and Aunt Marcia had to reassure her and help break her tension. Solemnly and seriously, at last understanding the importance of being a member of Christ's body, she partook of the sacrament. At our next lesson, she told me she giggled a little bit, and pointed to her heart. It was her spontaneous joy in expressing in a concrete way that she belonged to Jesus.

* * * * * * * * * * * * * * * * * * *

Lori loved to be scheduled for nursery at church. She confided to me that sometimes she liked nursery better than the sermon. She had an innate knack for handling little ones, and they took to her. They seemed to sense that, with her handicap, she was special, and young children responded well to her. Even in the after-services fellowship in the halls of Byron Center Christian Junior High School, she made sure the younger children did not run in the halls. She also sensed when they were too noisy. She would say, for example, "Yonntun. . . shh!!" and Jonathan would look up in amazement and say, "How do you know I was noisy?" She would shake his shoulder playfully, but with a stern face, put her fingers to her lips, and "Yonntun" obeyed. I am not sure how she knew when a child raised his voice, but she knew!

However, babies were her first love. She was eagerly looking forward to the February birth of very special twins. We had with us in America for three years a seminary student and his wife from Singapore, Jaikishin and Esther Mahtani. Jaiki, an Indian by birth, and Esther, Chinese, lived across the road from our home, and were quickly learning our strange American customs. After Esther became pregnant and learned that she would have twins, Lori was ecstatic, for, as with everyone else, Lori wanted to be friends with the Singaporeans. After the twins, Jonathan and David, were born in February, Jaiki and Esther invited Lori over with us to see the twins. She conformed to their life-style and left her shoes at the door, Singapore-style, and soon was communicating with the Mahtanis.

But when she held the almond-eyed, olive-skinned, black-haired darlings by turn, she had eyes and arms only for the babies. Clumsy and uncoordinated as Lori could be, with babies she had just the right touch for handling them; and when Jaiki took her picture with the babies, her cup of joy almost ran over.

In the early summer, Lori made the acquaintance of another new baby, much closer to her. Debbie's baby, Justin, was born, and Lori had a nephew. As an aunt, Lori coddled him, pampered him, and loved him; and the talk time before our lessons usually included the latest news about Justin.

* *

During that springtime, Lori was coming at eleven a.m. on every other Saturday. Pastor Gritters and I were still alternating

lessons, and Saturday mornings worked well for both of us. It was even better for Lori, for she discovered that it was not very hard to get an invitation to stay for a noon lunch after the lesson was over, to drag out the clean-up chores, and stay as long as she could. We were finishing our work on the psalms by this time, and I decided to teach her the third area of instruction I had planned: God's revelation to us of the last things.

I asked her some introductory questions one morning: "Do you know that God tells us in His Word what will happen before the end of the world? Do you know how God will destroy the world?"

Lori's answers to all my questions were no. I wrote a note on the board telling her that she should know what God's plan for the future is; and that our next set of lessons would teach her about it. Lori studied the doctrine of the last things with me until our lessons ended in May.

With her quick comprehension of time relationships, Lori was able to understand how many years had gone by since God had created our world. And if she had the knowledge and background of the history of the world up to the present, I could go on to the prophecies of the Book of Revelation.

Our first lesson started with a review. Her lesson told her: "You learned already that God made His whole world in six days, Lori."

She gave me her crooked smile when she remembered her excitement the day she had learned about it. We went on: "Next, God put many people in His world. There were always *two* kinds of people living on this earth: God's people and the devil's people. Another way of saying it is: the righteous people and the wicked people. It is important to remember this. Cain was wicked. Abel was righteous. All through the Bible stories that you read, you have found God's people and the devil's people.

In the Old Testament part of the Bible, God's people lived in the land of Canaan. All this time, God's people were waiting for someone special to be born. Who was it?" _____

Lori answered, "Jesus or John."

"Why?" I motioned, pointing to John.

"John — beloved Son — baptize — tell people — Matt. 3:17" went up on the chalkboard.

I might have known. Lori could never forget John the Baptist, Jesus' forerunner. He meant much to Lori. He was the one who showed her Jesus; and he was her friend, she once told me. John the Baptist *was* someone special! We read on in the lesson:

> The Old Testament part of the Bible lasted about 4,000 years. Can you think how long that is? It is something like living 100 years 40 times.
> Then, at the most important time of the world, someone special was born. Who was it? (Lori answered *Jesus*.) Jesus preached, you remember, and many people turned from their sins to worship and love the Lord. But the wicked people in the world hated Jesus, because He was God's Son, and they made Him die on the cross.
> After about 100 years, the Bible ended. God had told us all we need to know in His book. . . . God always had His church in all the countries of the world, and God always saw to it that there were preachers to preach His Word and to teach His people. After someone found out how to print books, everyone could easily get a Bible. . . .
> About 2000 more years have passed. 2000 + 4000 = _____ (Lori answered *6000*. She had no trouble with math.) The earth is about 6000 years old now. And the Bible tells His people all about the things that still have to happen. . . .
> In the Book of Revelation, the last book of the Bible, in chapter 6, He tells us that a white horse will ride through the world. It is not a white horse that you can see. That white horse is a picture of *Jesus*, Who rides, by His Spirit, through the world. When Jesus' Spirit rides through the world, He makes preachers preach His Word, and He gives His church *faith* in their hearts to believe it. He gives babies to mothers and fathers in the church and He gives those babies faith so they can grow up to be God's children, too. Remember, when the

Bible makes a picture of Jesus riding on a white horse, it is a picture of Jesus as *King*. He is the king of His church. Jesus will always keep His church on the earth until the end of the world.

In chapter 6 of Revelation, God tells us that a red horse will ride through the world, too. It is not a real horse. The red horse is a picture of *war* and fighting and death. When people are killed in wars, they bleed, and *blood* is *red*. God tells us there will always be wars on this earth. . . .

In chapter 6 of Revelation, God tells that a black horse rides through the world, too. It is not a real horse, but it is a picture of famine. Remember, famine is *not having enough to eat,* so people get sick and starve and die. God says that while some people starve, other people will be very rich. . . .

The last horse in Revelation 6 is a pale green horse, and this horse is a picture of death. Everyone must die sometime, but once in a while God sends bad sicknesses called *plagues* when many people die all at once. Some people starve to death. Others are killed in storms. And all the time, God is ruling over these four horses that are not real horses.

Lori was *so* quiet as she read through the lesson. She sighed heavily as we finished, and then began her eloquent motions with hands and face to tell me she would never have *dreamed* that God told us about those four horses that were not *real* horses.

When I asked her whether she was sure she understood, if she could have talked she would have dismissed me with a curt, "Of course."

Then I looked at my watch. It was past lunch time! Lori was glad it was late. It gave her a better chance of being invited to stay and help me prepare and eat it. She stayed, of course; and we took one of our prayer cards upstairs for Lori for devotions, and prepared lunch for *three*. With her gesture of ring finger, hair, and "Vite," she asked if she might go down to the lower level and summon him for lunch.

They came up boisterously, especially Lori. I sensed she was teasing. "What is she prancing for?" my husband asked.

"Ask Lori."

Lori grabbed a pencil and wrote, "horses that not horses," and shouted with laughter at his puzzled face. She wouldn't tell him and neither would I, because while we were getting lunch, we had planned to read Revelation 6:1-8, about the four horsemen, for devotions after our meal. So poor "Vite" was teased by his almost-daughter all during our lunch. He retaliated by trying to keep the goodies away from her: and if laughter aids digestion, we all had good digestion that noon.

When we read the Bible passage at the end of lunch, she was serious again, and our secret was out, and "Vite" knew what we had studied that morning.

For several weeks we studied God's revelation of things to come — in a simplified form for Lori — enough so that she would have an overview of God's plan for the future of this world and its end. When I taught her about the last things, I thought she would likely long outlive her grandmother-teacher, and might even experience some of the precursory signs of our Lord's return. In God's counsel and providence, that was not to be.

Then the school year was over, and we discontinued lessons for the summer months. Lori had had persistent and nagging coughs during the last part of the season, and when there was a let-up in her cough, she always told me her "sickness was finished." But the cough reappeared. A relaxing summer would be good for her.

Before we ended our season, we made our yearly trip to Grandville Fabric. This time Lori chose a lavender and blue print, with a bit of rose in it — the colors that somehow described Lori's personality. As usual, she came for fittings as often as possible, and treated Eunice somewhat as a sister, feeling full freedom in her home. And my husband and I often said to one another that if we could choose another daughter, it would be Lori. Her friends and neighbors, her grandparents, aunts and uncles felt the same way about her. They liked to have her around. She seemed to fit in and scatter cheer wherever she went.

139

Chapter 11

Lori's Last Year

Each Sunday Pastor Gritters made a sermon, and sometimes two, for Lori. They were condensations of the ones he was preaching that Lord's day. Many of Lori's sermons followed his sermons on the Heidelberg Catechism; and in that way, Lori had a thorough review of the lessons she had had the year before.

Her pastor asked her to do a variety of activities on her sermon sheets: copy the text, underline words with special meanings as he specified, fill in blanks and, of course, read the sermon. Sometimes the concepts were difficult, as for example in his sermon on our Mediator, as he explained to Lori how Jesus is both God and man. Fearful, I suppose, that Lori might not be able to grasp the explanation, he wrote on the back page, "How was it?" and she answered, "Duck soup." She and I had tossed that phrase around quite often during our years of lessons, and she had used it that July afternoon a year earlier when her pastor first observed one of our lessons. After that, she and Pastor Gritters batted the phrase back and forth. At least she got the message across that she understood his sermon!

In her extensive notebook of sermons, her answers, her underlining, and her little notes proved that she was a very able "listener" with her eyes.

During her last year, Lori also grew in the art of prayer. Through that year Pastor Gritters often asked her, at the end of the sermon sheet, to make a prayer, and he gave her specific instructions. He wrote on one of his sermons: "Lori, make a prayer. Write what you feel in your heart." She did. In her broken style she wrote:
> "Lori write sermon church
> Lori will go to church
> Lori love for Gods church
> Lori's God gave us Lord's Supper."

141

When she was asked at the end of a sermon to thank the Lord, she wrote, "Lori write thank you a paper sermon." Frequently that unique phrase entered her sermon sheet, usually with a "Thanks for Rev. Gritters. Makes paper sermons."

For her prayers of thanks, Pastor Gritters left many blanks, for Lori had so many things for which she wanted to thank the Lord. He instructed on her sheet: "Thank God for:" (and Lori filled in)

> "the angels (which she spelled 'anglies')
> Jesus Christ on cross
> bread and wine
> I love God
> thank God for friends at church
> Mrs. Gritters talked to Lori at church (she loved the special attention)
> Debbi went a born a baby — Butterwroth — boy — name Justin"

When she made a prayer according to instructions on her sheet to "thank God for the Sabbath Day," she *could not* do it without including her family and friends.

> "Randy read the Bible
> Lori study your paper sermons
> Lenny study your catechism
> Tom read books about the Bible"

I think that sometimes Lori's prayers of thanks and her ideas of proper sabbath observance were a bit jumbled, but she had the idea of doing what was right and thanking God for the privilege.

Characteristically, when Pastor Gritters gave her instructions to "praise God," she wrote:

> "Sky is God's
> Trees belong to God
> All the animals"

She loved to emphasize that all nature sings His praises!

142

Her answers to questions on her paper sermons were specific. In answer to her pastor's question: "Do you pray at night in bed?" she wrote, "Yes — 9:30."

And in the last sermon in her notebook, she was the loving, outgoing Lori, as usual. She wrote, with instructions to pray for *others:* "God likes us to pray for our friends."

In her prayer life, she met her Lord as a simple, yet profound Lori, who loved her Lord and her fellow saints, who enjoyed simple pleasures and gave hearty thanks, all with profound understanding.

* *

After a summer vacation, from lessons, too, Lori and I took up our work again in September. This season we would study the Book of Acts. It was breaking new ground for Lori. We had ended her first year of lessons three years ago with the resurrection of our Lord, and had never gotten to the study of the history of the spread of the gospel through the apostles.

In introduction, I wrote to Lori:

> Lori, when I taught you at Hudsonville, we did not learn any more about Jesus, because we did not have any more time. But the Bible tells us very much more, and because you are one of God's dear children, you will want to learn about it. Right? Do you know what Jesus did after He came out of the grave? For *40* days, He came and visited His children here on the earth. They did not see Jesus all the time, but sometimes He came right into the room where they were sitting. Even when the doors and windows were locked, Jesus would suddenly be in the room. How can that be? Because Jesus had a special body, and He could come into the room without going through the door. When Jesus came to His friends, the disciples, we say He *appeared* to them. The Bible tells us about the *ten* times that Jesus *appeared* to His disciples, and then it was time for Jesus to go back to heaven to live. We call it Jesus' *ascension,* and His disciples were there with Him on the Mount of Olives when a cloud took Jesus to heaven.

After the introduction, in following lessons we studied Pentecost, the preaching of Peter and John, and the martyrdom of Stephen. True to her character, Lori was very angry with the Jews who persecuted the new Christian church, and with Saul who held the coats of the men who stoned Stephen.

And then we came to the story of Cornelius.

Our lesson told us that: "In chapter 10, the Bible takes us in verse 1 to Caesarea. Find Caesarea on the map. *Cornelius* lived there. He came from the country of Italy."

Before we read the next words: "Find Italy on the map," Lori said, "Boot." She reached for the atlas and found the boot-shaped Italy, and figured how many miles Cornelius had to travel to get to Palestine.

Back to the lesson again, she read, "Cornelius was *not* an Israelite. When Cornelius was younger, he did not believe in Jesus. He was a *centurion.* That means he was a captain over one hundred men in the army, and he lived in Israel. He had heard about Jesus; and God touched his heart, and he believed. He was *devout.* Find the word in verse 2. *Devout* means that he loved the Lord. He prayed much and helped poor people. Would you have liked Cornelius?"

Lori answered, "Yes."

That was verse 2. I put up three fingers to let her know that we would go on to the next verse. But Lori shook her head, picked up the chalk, and wrote "Devout" on the board. Underneath she wrote: "Love God and love neighbor. Two tables of law."

I was proud of my Lori! She understood how a devout Christian lives. What word would best show my happiness with her insight? I wrote, "Great, Lori!"

Calmly she erased my praise, and I motioned again to go on to

144

verse 3. No, she was not ready. She began bordering the board with "Love — Love — Love" all around the edges, as she had often done before, and printed "Mrs. Hoekeman" next to the word "Devout." Then, "teaches girls — writes Bible Story Book."

I thanked her and hugged her and, settled back in my chair, put up three fingers: shall we go on to verse 3?

No. She erased everything on the board except the "Loves" and the "Devout," and printed, "Mr. Hoekeman. Teaches in Christian School for ministers," and in a corner of the board, in small letters, "Lenny Holstege," her cousin, and a student in pre-seminary.

Touched by Lori's double tribute, I hugged her again, and this time lipped to her, "Verse 3 now?"

No. She made her sign of knocking and kissing, and started for the study. I followed.

"What's it all about *now?*" my husband asked, looking at Lori's crooked grin. When would he remember to expect the un-expected from her?

"Ask Lori."

She was already pulling him into the hall. He *must* read what she had written.

In her way, this unusual girl explained to "Vite" how we had arrived at this display, and read verse 2 with him so that he would understand. . . and Lori was hugged a third time.

After he left, I put up three fingers once more, and a nonchalant Lori nodded, as if there had been no interruption.

* *

The rest of our season we devoted to Lori's lessons about Paul. She followed his missionary journeys with the atlas at her side, and for each missionary journey she took home a map to do for her homework assignment. She loved the mapwork, and her maps came back beautifully done. We did not quite finish the history of Paul. We could not complete his journey to Rome near the end of his life.

Lori missed some lessons because of transportation problems and because of her health. In the spring especially the nagging cough was more frequent and it was not often that she could report, "Cough all finished."

I speculated whether her problems as a severe diabetic were bothering her more lately. She seemed more slow than usual. I had noticed it already back in December, when we had our craft party at Hudsonville Church with the other girls, and made magnets for our mothers' refrigerators. She did a lovely job of painting and decorating her tongue depressor and clip clothespin for the magnet, but she fell asleep while the other girls were finishing and doing the clean-up. The girls were concerned. Betty thought she didn't act like Lori today, and I thought so, too. We gave her some candy, because it seemed as if it could be a bit of an insulin reaction, but Lori did not perk up much. She slept most of the way home.

Through the early springtime months she had ups and downs of feeling well and feeling "bad." She was still tired very often, and because transportation was a problem at that time, too, we discontinued our lessons in April of 1986.

The problem was more serious than we knew.

146

Chapter 12

Lori Goes Home

We saw one another only occasionally during the summer. It was not a summer like the last three summers had been!

On Monday afternoon, August 25, Grandma Holstege called: "Lori is in the hospital. The doctors don't know what her problem is. We thought it was her diabetes again, but she had lots of doctors around her, and they are talking possible kidney failure," she said. "It doesn't look so good.

"She's real good about all the tests, but she feels rather miserable. Can you come to see her?"

We talked a few minutes longer, and I hung up, stunned by the news. The telephone rang again. It was Lori's father this time.

"I've been trying to get you. Your line was busy," he said.

"I was talking with your mom. I know about Lori being in the hospital."

He wanted to talk about Lori. She had not felt very well all summer. She did not have the zest she usually did for summer activities. Swimming was her favorite recreation during the summertime. Anyone who knew Lori knew that! But the last weeks she had not felt like swimming.

On Saturday afternoon she wanted to go to the horse pulls with the rest of her family. Her father advised her to stay at home because she did not seem to be well, but Lori insisted she was all right.

When she started to throw up at the horse pulls, her father took her home. She was sick all through the night. On Sunday noon her father took her to the hospital.

My husband and I went to the hospital early Monday evening. Before we left, I picked the prettiest roses from the rose garden, arranged them as tastefully as I could, but not up to Lori's standard, of course, and we took them along to Butterworth Hospital.

When we came to her room, her bed was empty. A friendly nurse told us to go down to the visitor's room next to the heart catherization lab on Floor A and meet her family there.

We looked at one another. I think my husband's heart was pounding as hard and fast as mine. We said nothing, but somehow, we knew. We arrived at the visitor's room just as a doctor started to talk to the family. We were invited to step in and listen.

We heard him say, "pulmonary hypertension." My heart sank. We knew what that was: High blood pressure of the pulmonary artery.

The doctor talked quietly on: . . . it is usually congenital. . . she probably has lived with this for some time. . . the lungs do not get enough blood from the heart. . . all the organs of her body in turn suffer. . . no more testings or blood samples. . . will make her as comfortable as possible. . . very little hope of surviving long. . . she is being given oxygen. . . she will be transferred to her room. . . the family may see her soon. . . .

That was about all.

A quiet and weeping family filed out of the room. My husband took me aside and said quietly, "Translated, the doctor is telling us that she will die tonight." I nodded. I understood his words that way, too.

Pastor Gritters was out of town; and because of our close relationship with Lori, my husband, as minister, was asked to stay

148

for a while. Soon the nurse told the family they might see Lori in her room. She was conscious, but periodically lapsing into semi-consciousness, and breathing heavily. Some of the relatives went in. Some hesitated. I held back. Although I *felt* as if I were a relative, I was only a friend; but my husband, who had been asked to step into the room, came out to me, and said, "I was able to reach her. Come in and talk to her. I know you'll be able to reach her."

Still hesitant, I walked in, stroked her arm as I had so often done in the past four years, and she opened her eyes and gave her gesture of recognition: a quick flip of her hand. Then she looked at what I had in my hands: the roses. I had forgotten I was carrying them; and she gave me her sweet, crooked smile that said, "You still remembered."

When Lori was fully settled in, my husband prayed with the family. He prayed a prayer we were waiting to hear — not a prayer for her recovery — for she would not get better, but a prayer of thanks for Lori's testimony in her confession and in her life that she belonged to her faithful Savior, Jesus Christ; and he committed her into the arms of Jesus.

At eleven o'clock that night Lori went to be with Jesus.

The next day my husband and I were working together on a library project in his study. Both of us were very quiet that day. After we had been working silently for a time, I asked, "Do you think it is possible to be sad and glad at the same time?"

He thought so. I felt that way. I was sad. I felt sad for her family and relatives who would miss a very special girl so much. I felt sad for myself. No more lessons. No more hugs and kisses and nonsense. No more beautiful spiritual testimonies, not here on earth.

"If any child other than our own could have been our daughter, it would have been Lori," I muttered. We had said that before, but it showed how much we would miss her.

At the same time I was glad. I thought of one of our first lessons, the one about Jesus changing water to wine at the wedding in Cana, and how Lori understood that the wine was a picture of the joys of heaven, where she would have a perfect body, without deafness; and how she had written, "I be very happy."

I remembered what a struggle she had to join in the singing with the rest of God's people in the worship services, and could not really participate and enjoy it completely; and then I remembered that the first songs Lori ever heard were the songs of the angels — last night here — and timelessly in heaven. They were the songs of the angels she was so interested in when she lived with us here on the earth.

And I looked back to the day when she once told me in naive confidence: "Like Rev. Gritters very much — handsome — very good to Lori — nice man," and then, wistfully, "Talk nice?"

She had not complained, but she would have loved to hear his voice as he taught her in class and as he preached to her in church. Now she would hear another voice, saying, "Well done, good and faithful servant: enter thou into the joy of thy Lord."

* *

At the funeral home, banks of floral pieces, tributes from Lori's many friends and relatives, lined the room. The flowers, with their sweet scents, indelibly associated with funeral homes, formed the background for the lines of Lori's quiet and saddened friends.

In the casket lay only a shell of Lori. We knew that the real Lori is in heaven, singing praises. Lori had died. Soon the

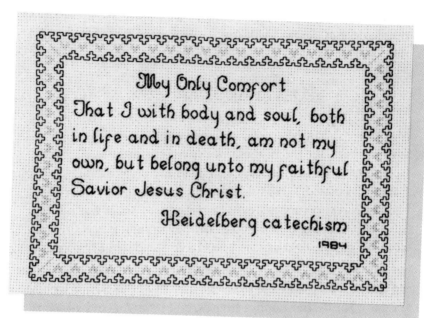

My Only Comfort
That I with body and soul, both
in life and in death, am not my
own, but belong unto my faithful
Savior Jesus Christ.
Heidelberg catechism
1984

flowers surrounding her would die, as all living things on this earth do. But in the casket with Lori was something that would never die. On a carefully embroidered counted cross-stitch sampler, made and given to Lori when she made confession of faith by friends, were stitched the words of Lori's enduring confession:

My Only Comfort
That I, with body and soul, both in life and in death
am not my own, but belong unto my faithful Savior,
Jesus Christ.

Since her confession two years earlier, the sampler always had a place in the headboard of her bed; and she told me, and her pastor, that every night before she went to bed, she read it and hugged it (of course) before she prayed her evening prayer. It is Lori's enduring confession to all eternity.

The funeral service was on Thursday. Pastor Gritters preached from a psalm Lori loved, and about one of her favorite concepts in Scripture: Christ as her Shepherd. His words were based on verse 4 of Psalm 23: "Yea, though I walk through the valley of the shadow of death, I will fear no evil: for thou art with me; thy rod and thy staff they comfort me."

My husband, asked to take the committal service at the graveside, chose to read two texts with his brief remarks. The first, Matthew 3:17, was not ordinarily an appropriate text for a time such as this. But today these words were appropriate: "And lo, a voice from heaven, saying, This is my beloved Son, in whom I am well pleased." He told us at the graveside that he read it because it was certainly Lori's favorite text: for it was her first full understanding of the Son as her Savior, and it was the text from which, she told us two years later, she dated her conversion.

He closed with a message from the mouth of our Savior which for Lori, for us, her family, friends, and relatives, and all who share her faith, left us with the only comfort in life and in death. He read John 11:25, 26: "Jesus said unto her, I am the resurrection and the life: he that believeth in me, though he were dead, yet shall he live. And whosoever liveth and believeth in me shall never die."

The next Sunday, Lori's friends and relatives from her congregation of Byron Center read these words of comfort on their bulletins:

"Late Monday night the Lord took Lori Holstege home to the glorious presence of her Lord. She died suddenly of cardio-pulmonary hypertension, a rare disease that sometimes strikes young women. We mourn her loss: not as those who have no hope, but as those who believe Lori is now in glory with the saints gone on before, waiting the Lord's return to take the rest of the church to be with them. We pray God's abundant mercy for the family to sustain them in this great trial.

'Yea, though I walk through the valley of the shadow of death, I will fear no evil, *for Thou art with me.*' "

The Lord took her through the valley of death to be with Him so she could say her favorite words to all eternity: "I belong to Jesus."